Animalium

For James
K. S.

For Edwin, lover of facts
J. B.

With thanks to Katie Cunningham
and Valerie Davies

Text and design copyright © 2014 by The Templar Company Limited
Illustrations copyright © 2014 by Katie Scott
Written by Jenny Broom

Publisher's note: Statistics on the size of species cited in these texts are mean averages
taken from data currently available.

First U.S. edition 2014

Library of Congress Catalog Card Number 2013952848
ISBN 978-0-7636-7508-0

14 15 16 17 18 19 CCP 10 9 8 7 6 5 4 3 2

Printed in Shenzhen, Guangdong, China

This book was typeset in Gill Sans and Mrs Green.
The illustrations were done in pen and ink and colored digitally.

BIG PICTURE PRESS
an imprint of
Candlewick Press
99 Dover Street
Somerville, Massachusetts 02144

www.candlewick.com
www.bigpicturepress.net

Welcome
to the
Museum

ENTER HERE

Animalium

illustrated by KATIE SCOTT

written by JENNY BROOM

BPP

Preface

Earth is the only planet we know about so far that has life on it, and the life-forms that make their home here have evolved to become both numerous and diverse. We share our planet with about two million other species of living things—and these are just the ones we know about and have given names to.

This variety of life is called biodiversity, and although that idea might seem abstract and not part of our daily lives, it is actually what keeps the earth a good place for us to live. And since humans are a species of animal—just like flies or jellyfish or giraffes—we too are part of biodiversity.

The variety of animals on Earth is amazing. Most are insects, and very small, and some are so odd, you couldn't make them up! But while they might look strange to us, they all have a role in making the earth a fit place to live. The diversity of life on Earth is what sustains us—without it, there would be no food for us to eat or air to breathe.

Every species plays a part in the web of life, and I hope we can imagine and make real a future in which humankind shares this planet more fairly and effectively with the wondrous and life-sustaining diversity of creatures that call it home.

You'll get an overview of that diversity in this book, with galleries featuring examples of the extraordinary, odd, and beautiful creatures we share this planet with. I hope it fascinates and inspires you.

Dr. Sandra Knapp
Natural History Museum, London, England

Entrance

Welcome to Animalium

This museum is like none you've ever visited before. It's open twenty-four hours a day, seven days a week, and its collection boasts a fascinating catalog of the world's creatures, with each exhibit in immaculate condition and presented in fantastic detail.

Wander through the pages of the museum to tour its galleries and see the story of life on Earth unfold. Each chapter represents a different gallery of the museum, focusing on one class of animal, such as reptiles, birds, or mammals. The classes are arranged in evolutionary order to show how the animal kingdom has developed over time. See for yourself how the tree of life evolved from the simple sea sponge into the diverse array of animals found on Earth today.

Pause to inspect each exhibit carefully. Some rooms showcase a group of related animals; look for characteristic similarities and read the text to find out more about how the animals are comparable. Some galleries offer a glimpse of the museum's dissection laboratory, where the animals' skeletons and internal organs can be studied.

In addition, each gallery includes a habitat diorama, showcasing an ecosystem and the animals who live there. See how different climates support different ecosystems, and learn how species have evolved over millions of years to become perfectly adapted to their surroundings.

This is the only museum to house animals ancient and modern, enormous and tiny, vicious and vulnerable, between two covers. So enter *Animalium* and see the animal kingdom in all its glory.

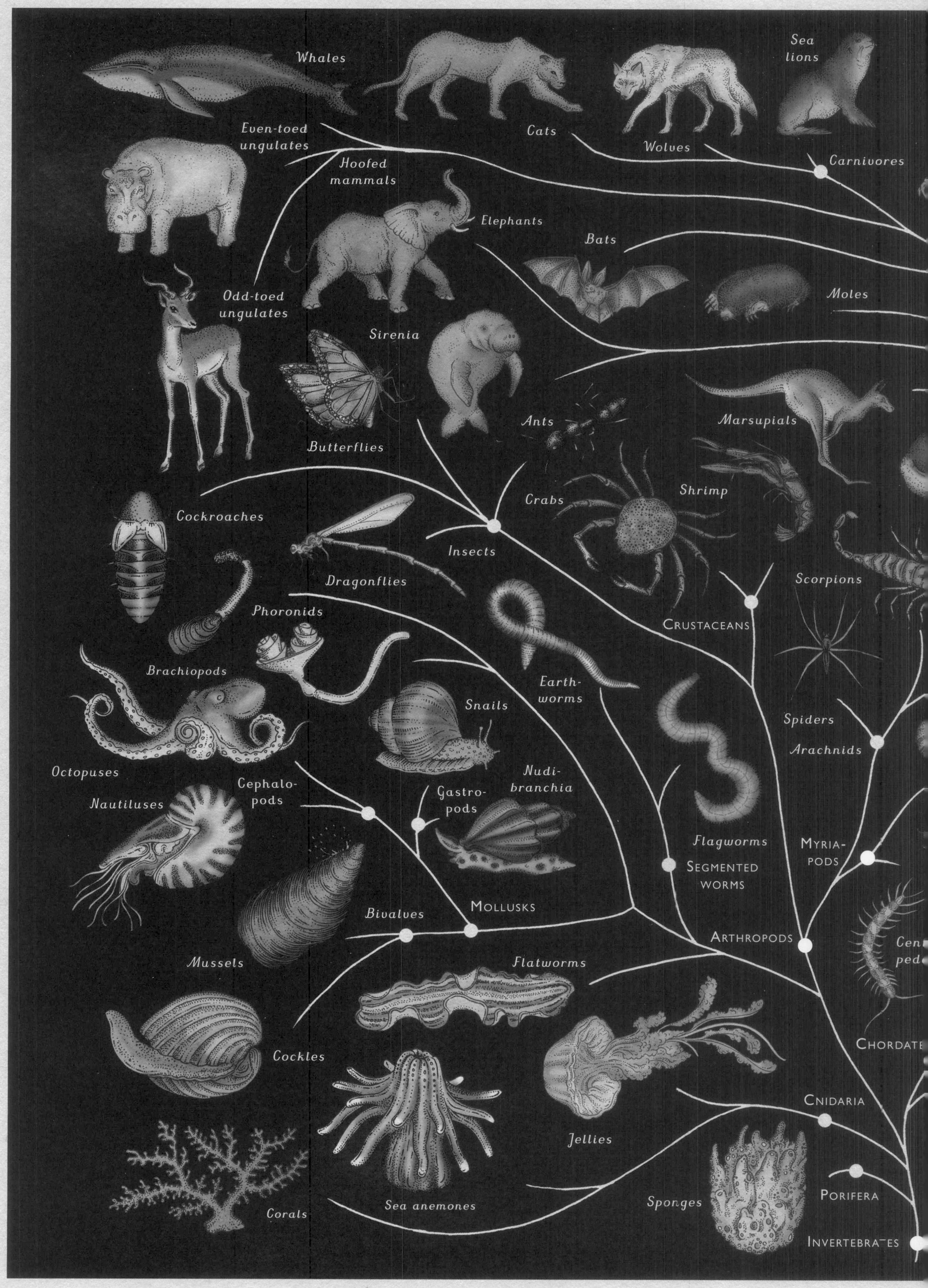

Whales

Even-toed
ungulates

Hoofed
mammals

Cats

Wolves

Sea
lions

Carnivores

Elephants

Bats

Moles

Odd-toed
ungulates

Sirenia

Ants

Marsupials

Butterflies

Crabs

Shrimp

Cockroaches

Insects

Scorpions

Dragonflies

CRUSTACEANS

Phoronids

Earth-
worms

Brachiopods

Snails

Spiders

Arachnids

Octopuses

Cephalo-
pods

Gastro-
pods

Nudi-
branchia

Nautiluses

Flagworms

MYRIA-
PODS

SEGMENTED
WORMS

Bivalves

MOLLUSKS

ARTHROPODS

Mussels

Flatworms

Cen-
ped.

CHORDATE

Cockles

CNIDARIA

Jellies

Corals

Sea anemones

Sponges

PORIFERA

INVERTEBRATES

Humans

Apes

Lemurs

Monkeys

Kiwis
and ratites

Penguins

Parrots and
cockatoos

Primates

Rodents

BIRDS

Crocodiles
and alligators

Birds of
prey

Rabbits

Placentals

Lizards

Storks, ibises,
and herons

Snakes

Egg-laying
monotremes

Reptiles

Turtles and
tortoises

Amphibians

Mammals

Urodela

Lungfish

Frogs
and toads

Newts
and salamanders

Mites

Lobe-finned
fish

Millipedes

Salmon and
trout

Cartilaginous
fish

Ray-finned
fish

Carp and
goldfish

Jawless fish

Sharks

Lampreys

Skates and rays

VERTEBRATES

Sea squirts

Larvaceans

Lancelets

TUNICATES

ECHINODERMS

Sea urchins

Brittle stars

Starfish

The Tree
of Animal Life

Crinoids

Sea cucumbers

The Tree of Life

The tree of life is a lot like a family tree. It encompasses all of the animals on the planet and shows how each group is related. It visualizes, on a very basic level, how organisms that appear to be very different have, in fact, evolved from one another over millions of years.

Charles Darwin illustrated the tree of life in his book *On the Origin of Species* in 1859, in which he concluded that all life on Earth was related and descended from a common ancestor. Since that time, we've broadened our understanding of genetics, biochemistry, and DNA, and those scientific endeavors indicate that Charles Darwin was probably right about a lot of his ideas. Modern science indicates that eukaryotes—organisms whose cells have a clearly defined nucleus—such as animals, plants, algae, and fungi, do appear to share a common ancestor.

The earliest—and simplest—organism is located at the base of the tree of life. As species have evolved, adapting to survive in particular habitats, they are shown on the diagram to branch away from the original stem. Hence, the farther a species is located from this base point, the more evolutionary modifications it has undergone.

These adaptations happen gradually over many generations. Characteristics that give an animal an advantage in its chosen environment increase its chances of surviving and reproducing, and thus of passing its genes on to its offspring. This theory, known as natural selection, lets us understand how the millions of species on Earth today have come into being over time.

Gallery 1

Invertebrates

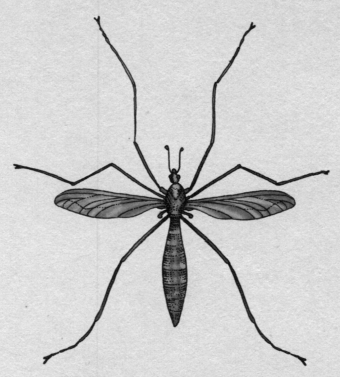

Invertebrates

Invertebrates are grouped together not because they all share significantly similar features but because they all lack one: a jointed spine, or backbone. The term *vertebrate* comes from the Latin word *vertebra*, meaning "joint," particularly of the spine. And *in* is Latin for "not." *Invertebrate* therefore means "without a jointed spine."

The term *invertebrate* refers to animals from across several evolutionary branches that in some cases are only very distantly related. Consequently, invertebrates vary widely, from the simple sponge to the complex and intelligent octopus.

Most invertebrates evolved around 540 million years ago, making them Earth's earliest animals. And while vertebrates—those species that evolved to have a jointed spine—often outdo their spineless cousins in size and intelligence, invertebrates come out ahead in numbers, making up around 97 percent of the animal kingdom. Their successful evolution story means that they can be found almost everywhere on Earth: in water, in the air, on land, and even underground.

Invertebrates can be divided into related groups, which include sponges, Cnidaria (such as jellyfish), flatworms, segmented worms, mollusks (including cockles and mussels as well as octopuses and squid), arthropods (including insects, arachnids, and crustaceans), and echinoderms (such as starfish).

Porifera

Porifera, or sponges, are thought to be the first phylum, or overarching category of animal, to evolve from the earliest life-forms, single-celled creatures called protozoa. Fossils found in southern Australia suggest that sponges were living in the waters there up to 665 million years ago. The evolution of the multicellular sponge all those millions of years ago was one of the most significant developments in natural history.

Living exclusively underwater, sponges can be found in all habitats, from tropical seas to icy waters. With no nervous system or organs, sponges are incapable of thought or movement, and it would be easy to mistake them for plants. However, sponges are in fact animals that feed on bacteria and sense and react to their environments.

Although they come in many shapes, colors, and sizes, sponges all have structures based around a hollow central cavity (a bit like a chimney) surrounded by several small holes. This design allows water to flow through the sponge's central channel, nourishing it with food and oxygen and carrying away carbon dioxide. Some sponges contain chemicals with medicinal properties, which make them useful to humankind.

Key to plate

1: Cross section of bath sponge
Spongia officinalis
Length: 14 inches/35 centimeters
This sponge is found predominantly in Greek waters at depths of up to 130 feet/40 meters.

2: Calcareous sponge
Leucosolenia botryoides
Length: 1/2 inch/1.5 centimeters
This species grows in a mass of free-standing branches sometimes likened to bunches of bananas.

3: Bath sponge
Spongia officinalis
Length: 14 inches/35 centimeters
See caption 1, above. This soft and porous sponge is grown commercially and sold for bathing use.

4: Stove-pipe sponge
Aplysina archeri
Length: 45 inches/114 centimeters
These long, purple cylindrical sponges grow in large groups of up to twenty-two tubes. They sway with the water's current.

5: Orange fan sponge
Stylissa flabelliformis
Length: 1 foot/30 centimeters
This species gets its name from its resemblance to a paper folding fan. It grows on rocky shelves.

6: Yellow finger sponge
Callyspongia ramosa
Length: 1 foot/30 centimeters
This sponge is found in waters around New Zealand. Its extracts are useful to the pharmaceutical industry.

7: Venus's flower basket sponge
Euplectella aspergillum
Length: 17 inches/43 centimeters
The silicon spicules that form this sponge's skeleton fuse together into a kind of brittle and delicate natural glass.

8: Purse sponge
Grantia compressa
Length: 6 inches/15 centimeters
This small, bulbous sponge has a smooth surface and an elongated neck, making it resemble a gourd.

9: Giant barrel sponge
Xestospongia muta
Diameter: 7 feet/2 meters
This slow-growing sponge can reach large dimensions, which suggests that it may live for a hundred years or more.

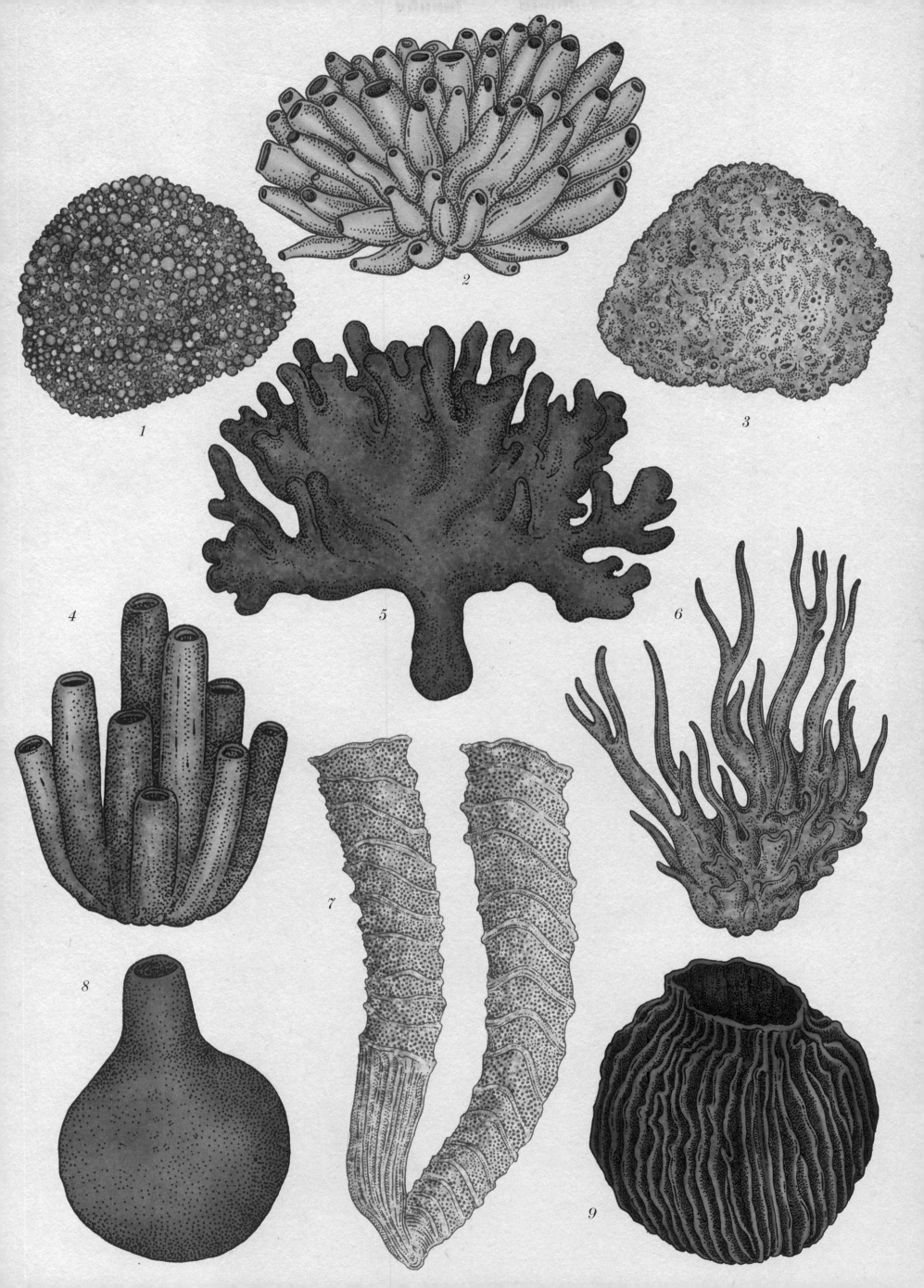

Cephalopods

The cephalopod family is an ancient form of marine life that once dominated the seas. There are now around 800 species in this class, and they can be found in every ocean.

The word *cephalopod* means "head-foot" in Greek, which reflects their anatomy. Their size is recorded by the length of their body cavity, called a mantle, which sits behind the head. They have large brains and advanced senses, making them sociable creatures able to communicate with one another. They sometimes even shoal with fish for company.

Cephalopods can change the color and pattern of their bodies to camouflage

themselves or ward off predators. They have sucker-like tentacles, and move by taking in water and shooting it out to propel themselves forward.

Cephalopods produce ink, and when threatened, they release an inky cloud to confuse predators. Some can produce an ink cloud that is similar in size, shape, and color to their own body, which acts as a decoy and gives the cephalopod a chance to escape.

───────────────── *Key to plate* ─────────────────

1: Long-armed squid
Chiroteuthis veranyi
Mantle: 5 inches/13 centimeters
This slow-moving squid lives at depths around 1 1/2 miles/2.4 kilometers.

2: Whip-lash squid
Mastigoteuthis microlucens
Mantle: 4 inches/10 centimeters
The long, whip-like tentacles of this squid are covered in tiny, sticky suckers.

3: Angel octopus
Velodona togata
Mantle: 6 inches/15 centimeters
This deep-sea octopus lives at depths of up to 2,000 feet/700 meters.

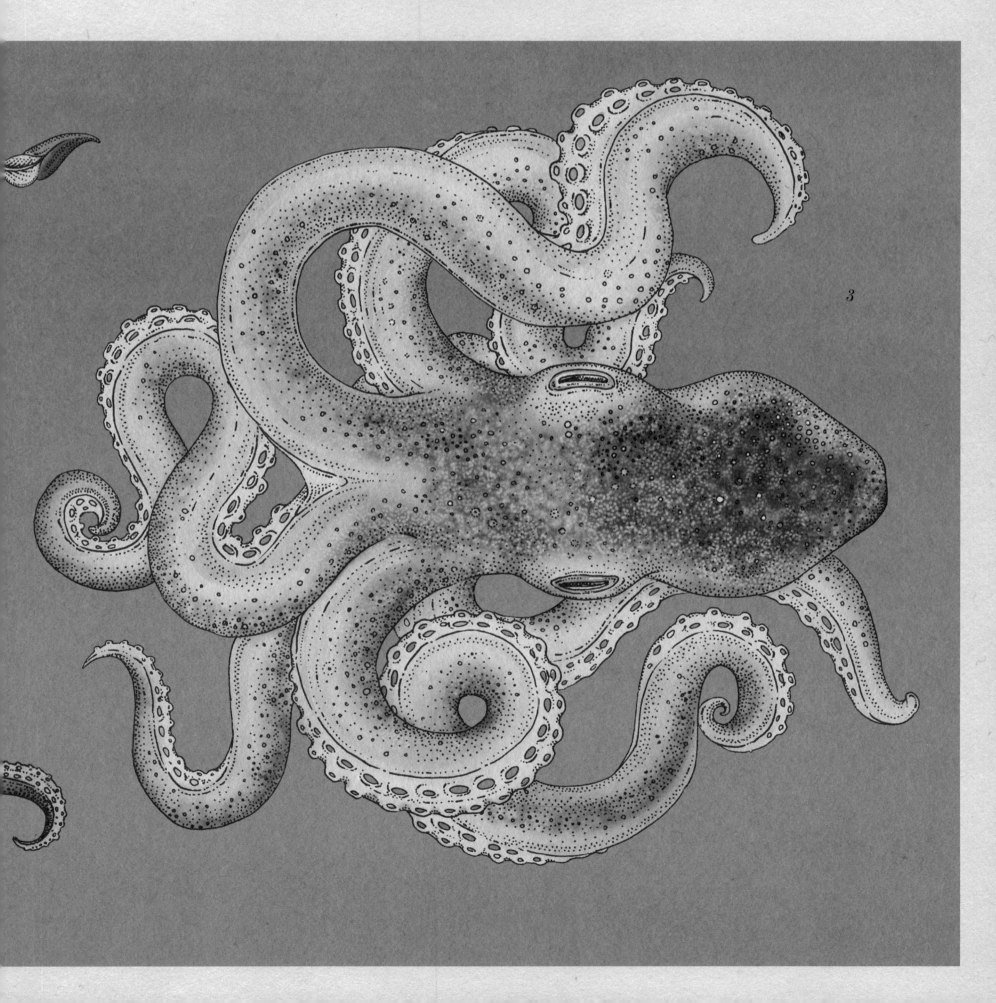

Cnidaria

There are over 10,000 known cnidarian species, and they come in widely diverse forms. Some, such as sea anemones and corals, are static polyps, which means they attach themselves to rocks. Others, such as the box jelly, move around on their own by contracting their bodies.

Despite looking different, these species are uniformly aquatic and all have a decentralized nervous system, with no brain or heart. All cnidarians also share the ability to sting. In fact, their name comes from the Greek word *knide,* which means "nettle." Cnidarians have inherited a harpoon-like stinger from a single common ancestor.

Cnidarians are carnivorous, meaning that they eat other animals in order to survive. Because they are not built to chase or hunt down their victims, they are known as "passive predators," meaning that they wait for other creatures to blunder into them. When unwitting prey brush past their tentacles, a hair-like trigger is activated, causing a toxic capsule to eject from the cnidarian's body and harpoon its victim. A cnidarian's sting can paralyze and kill its prey, and an unlucky encounter with the species can be extremely painful—and sometimes fatal—for humans, too.

―――――― *Key to plate* ――――――

1: **Black sea nettle**
Chrysaora achlyos
Diameter: 3 feet/1 meter
These giant jellyfish occasionally rise to the ocean's surface in enormous groups known as blooms.

2: **White-spotted jelly**
Phyllorhiza punctata
Diameter: 1½ feet/47 centimeters
Rather than catching live prey, this jellyfish filters up to 1,765 cubic feet/50 cubic meters of seawater per day to extract nutrients.

3: **Pacific sea nettle**
Chrysaora fuscescens
Diameter: 11 inches/28 centimeters
This jellyfish is covered in stinging cells called nematocysts, which embed tiny paralyzing barbs into their prey.

4: **Dahlia anemone**
Urticina felina
Diameter: 5 inches/13 centimeters
This sea anemone has up to 160 short tentacles around its mouth for catching prey like shrimp and fish.

5: **Staghorn coral**
Acropora cervicornis
Height: 7 feet/2 meters
The branches of this fast-growing coral are known to grow 4–8 inches/10–20 centimeters per year.

6: **Brain coral**
Diploria labyrinthiformis
Diameter: 7 feet/2 meters
At night, this coral extends its tentacles to catch passing prey. During the day, it wraps its tentacles around itself for protection.

7: **Stalked jelly**
Haliclystus stejnegeri
Height: 6 inches/15 centimeters
Rather than swimming freely like most other jellyfish, this species spends its entire life attached to rock or algae.

8: **Blue button jelly**
Porpita porpita
Diameter: 1 inch/2.5 centimeters
Despite its name, this is not a jelly but a colony of tiny organisms called zooids. Each has a unique job, such as digestion or defense.

9: **Flowerpot coral**
Goniopora djiboutiensis
Diameter: 3 feet/1 meter
This coral is so named because its polyps—with which it feeds—are arranged like the petals of a daisy.

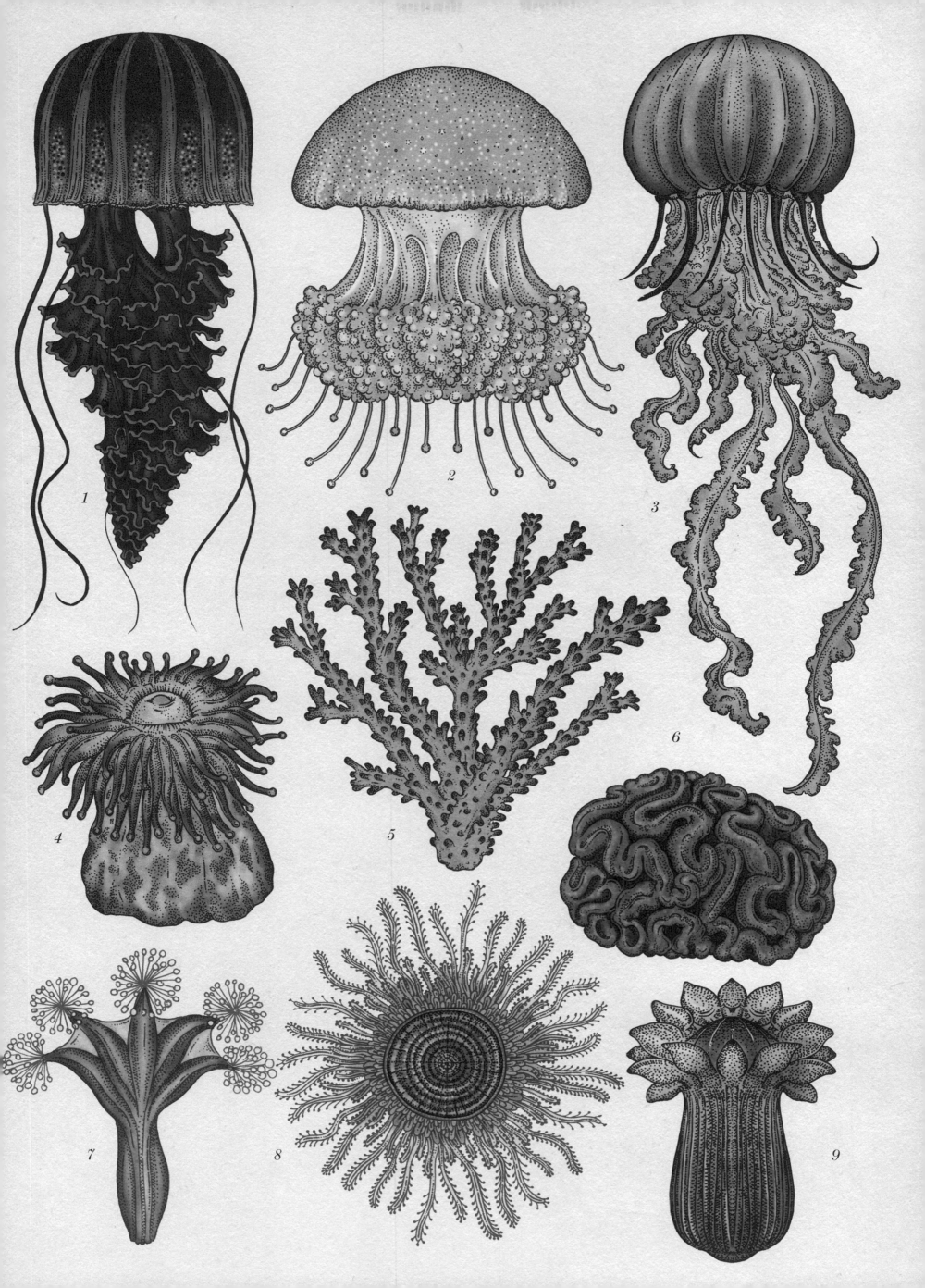

1

2

3

4

5

6

7

8

9

Flying Insects

Insects are an order of arthropod, making them closely related to crustaceans (crabs and lobsters), arachnids (spiders and scorpions), and myriapods (centipedes and millipedes). There are at least one million species of insects, making up over 80 percent of all living species on Earth. Around 10,000 new species are identified every year.

All arthropods have segmented bodies, jointed limbs, and exoskeletons, which are hard bodies with no internal bones. Insects today are small in size. However, some prehistoric dragonflies grew to have wingspans of up to 27 inches/70 centimeters.

Insects are the only invertebrates that have evolved to fly and were the first herbivores on Earth, eating a diet of only plants. Over millions of years, plants and insects have co-evolved, with plants finding ways to defend themselves from being eaten by insects while also relying on insects to spread their pollen to reproduce.

All insects experience a form of metamorphosis, gradually achieving maturity by undergoing a series of bodily changes. The changes experienced by the insect can be dramatic, with its body shape rendered almost unrecognizably different to its prior form. A well-known example is the transformation from caterpillar to butterfly.

Key to plate

1: Blue Mormon butterfly
Papilio polymnestor
Wingspan: 5 inches/13 centimeters
This butterfly is common in areas that experience heavy rainfall.

2: Crane fly
Tipula paludosa
Wingspan: 1 1/2 inches/4 centimeters
This nocturnal insect has long, delicate legs, which are easily detachable.

3: Mayfly
Ephemeroptera
Wingspan: 1/2 inch/1.5 centimeters
Mayflies live for just one hour.

4: Emperor dragonfly
Anax imperator
Length: 3 inches/7.5 centimeters
This species rarely lands.

5: Atlas moth
Attacus atlas
Wingspan: 1 foot/30 centimeters
This moth has the largest wings of any insect, but no mouth.

6: Pale snaketail dragonfly
Ophiogomphus severus
Length: 2 inches/5 centimeters
This species is rarely seen on cool days, preferring warmer temperatures.

7: Plains lubber grasshopper
Brachystola magna
Length: 2 inches/5 centimeters
This species can jump 3 feet/1 meter.

8: Luna moth
Actias luna
Wingspan: 4 inches/10 centimeters
This moth mimics fallen leaves.

9: Common green grasshopper
Omocestus viridulus
Length: 1 inch/2.5 centimeters
The characteristic noise made by this grasshopper is the sound of the male rubbing its hind legs together to attract a female mate.

10: Common wasp
Vespula vulgaris
Length: 1/2 inch/1.5 centimeters
When attacked, this aggressive wasp will send out an alarm to others to come and help.

11: Great black wasp
Sphex pensylvanicus
Length: 1 inch/2.5 centimeters
This wasp paralyzes its prey by stinging it, then carries it to an underground nest to feed its young.

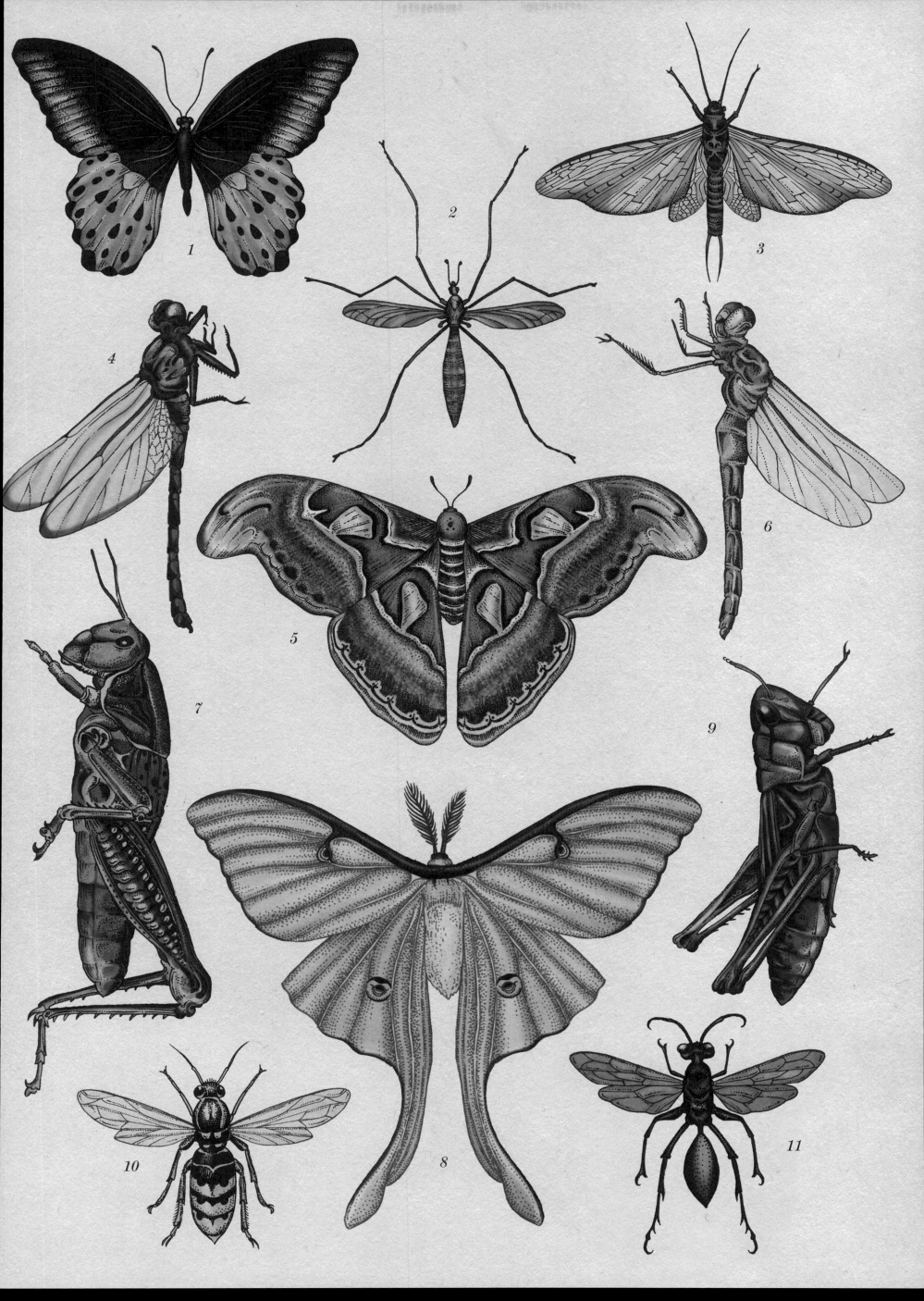

Habitat: Coastal Waters

Coastal habitats appear where the sea meets the land. There are about 221,208 miles/356,000 kilometers of coastline around the world, and the conditions there vary depending on the local climate, landscape, and turbulence of the ocean.

Coastal habitats are in constant flux as waves, tides, and currents drag water across the shores, meaning there is continuous change to the landscape. However, life in coastal areas is the most abundant in the world. This is because these habitats are rich in nutrients, which are delivered by rivers that flow into the sea and by waves' erosion of the land releasing minerals contained in the earth.

Many of the creatures that live in coastal waters, such as crabs, limpets, and scallops, are protected by hard shells, which help them to withstand battering waves. Some, such as mussels, are able to open their shells, sifting the water for food.

Some areas of the coast, known as intertidal zones, are above the water at low tide and below the water at high tide. This means that animals living in intertidal zones also face dramatic changes in temperature and varying water supplies, from fresh rainwater to saline seawater. Many species, such as barnacles, have cement glands that allow them to anchor themselves to a rock for stability as the tides rise and fall.

Key to plate

1: **Northern short-fin squid**
Illex illecebrosus
Mantle length: 5$\frac{1}{2}$ inches/14 centimeters

2: **Crown jelly**
Netrostoma setouchina
Diameter: 8 inches/20 centimeters

3: **Bushy-backed sea slug**
Dendronotus frondosus
Length: 4 inches/10 centimeters

4: **Calico crab**
Hepatus epheliticus
Width: 3 inches/7.5 centimeters

5: **Lettuce sea slug**
Elysia crispata
Length: 2 inches/5 centimeters

6: **Blue mussel**
Mytilus edulis
Length: 3 inches/7.5 centimeters

7: **True tulip snail**
Fasciolaria tulipa
Length: 5 inches/13 centimeters

8: **Calico scallop**
Argopecten gibbus
Length: 3 inches/7.5 centimeters

9: **Striped venus clam**
Chamelea gallina
Length: 1$\frac{1}{2}$ inches/4 centimeters
Often found buried in muddy sand.

10: **Little gray barnacle**
Chthamalus fragilis
Diameter: $\frac{1}{2}$ inch/1.5 centimeters
Can be hermaphroditic (both male and female).

11: **Cushion star**
Oreaster reticulatus
Diameter: 9 inches/23 centimeters
The juvenile is camouflaged green.

Gallery 2

Fish

Fish

Fish were the first vertebrates to evolve from invertebrates. They are cold-blooded and live in a variety of waters, from fresh to brackish to salty, and from freezing to tropical. Because there are 32,000 different species, there is a broader diversity of fish than any other type of vertebrate. There are four categories of fish: ancient jawless fish, such as lampreys; cartilaginous fish, such as sharks; common ray-finned fish with bony skeletons, such as tuna; and lobe-finned fish, such as lungfish, which are thought to be the ancestors of all land-dwelling animals. These four groups show the various evolutionary stages that fish have gone through over millions of years.

Most of the fish in the primitive jawless category are now extinct, but their notochord, a flexible rod down their back that formed a kind of rudimentary backbone, has an evolutionary legacy. It bridges the gap between the spineless invertebrates and their bony vertebrate descendants.

Eventually, around 395 million years ago, some lobe-finned fish evolved into tetrapods. Tetrapods adapted to breathe air and inhabit land for the very first time in Earth's history. This evolutionary leap gave rise to amphibians, reptiles, and, later, birds and mammals.

Key to plate

1: Red mullet
Mullus surmuletus
Length: 10 inches/25 centimeters
This ray-finned fish is a species of goat fish, so called because of the two sensory barbels that hang from its chin, which it uses to locate prey. Its color changes depending on its depth in the water and the time of day.

2: West Indian Ocean coelacanth
Latimeria chalumnae
Length: 5 feet/1.5 meters
Known as the "living fossil," this is the oldest-known living species of lobe-finned fish and is closely related to the lungfish. The coelacanth was thought to be extinct until one was caught in 1938. It is nocturnal and hides in caves throughout the day.

3: Sockeye salmon
Oncorhynchus nerka
Length: 28¹/₂ inches/72 centimeters
An adaptable species of ray-finned fish, the sockeye salmon spends its early life living in freshwater lakes before swimming out into the saline waters of the Pacific Ocean. In order to spawn, it swims upriver to its birthplace.

4: Sea lamprey
Petromyzon marinus
Length: 23 inches/60 centimeters
This ancient, primitive fish is jawless and appears to have evolved very little from the species that inhabited the seas 300 million years ago. It attaches itself to prey with its sucker-like mouth full of sharp teeth and then draws out the flesh of its victim.

5: Atlantic mackerel
Scomber scombrus
Length: 1 foot/30 centimeters
The most commonly found species of mackerel in British waters, this fast, streamlined ray-finned fish is known to perform long migrations. It forms huge shoals that swim close to the surface of the water.

6: Giant oarfish
Regalecus glesne
Length: 10 feet/3 meters
The narrow and ribbon-like, ray-finned oarfish holds the world record for the longest species of fish. It lives at depths of up to 3,000 feet/1,000 meters and is rarely seen alive. It swims by waving its body and rowing itself with its pelvic fins.

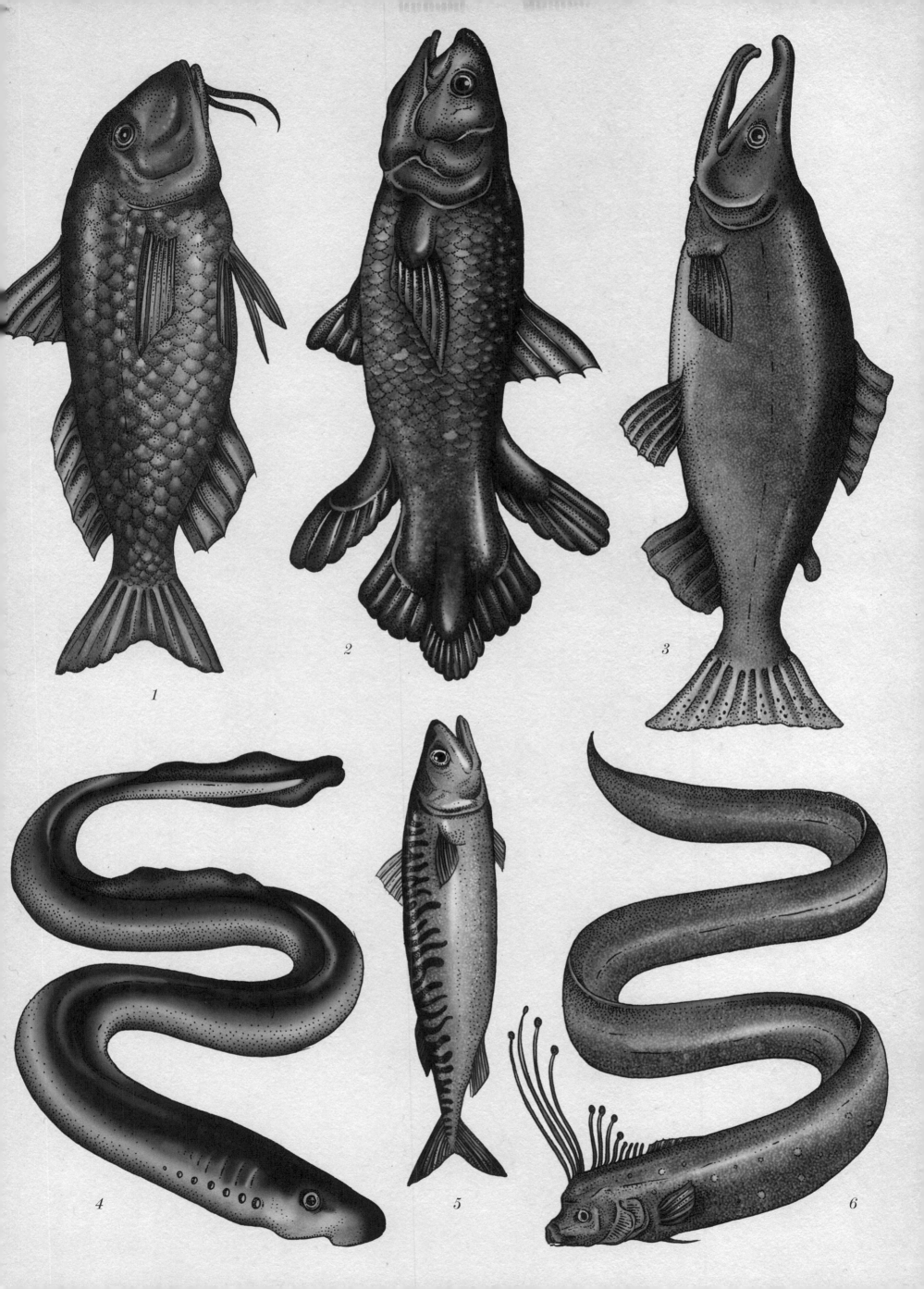

Sharks

Sharks evolved about 420 million years ago, and today there are more than 470 species. The world's largest predatory fish, the great white shark (*Carcharodon carcharias*, below), is among them. It reaches lengths of up to 20 feet/6.1 meters. Sharks are cartilaginous fish: instead of hard bone, they have supple cartilage, which makes their bodies light and flexible.

Unlike other fish, sharks have rough skin with dermal denticles rather than smooth scales, and while many lay eggs, some give birth to live young. They do not have a gas-filled bladder to stay buoyant in water; instead, they rely on their oily liver and dynamic lift to stay at the right depth, cruising through water as birds do in air. This means that most

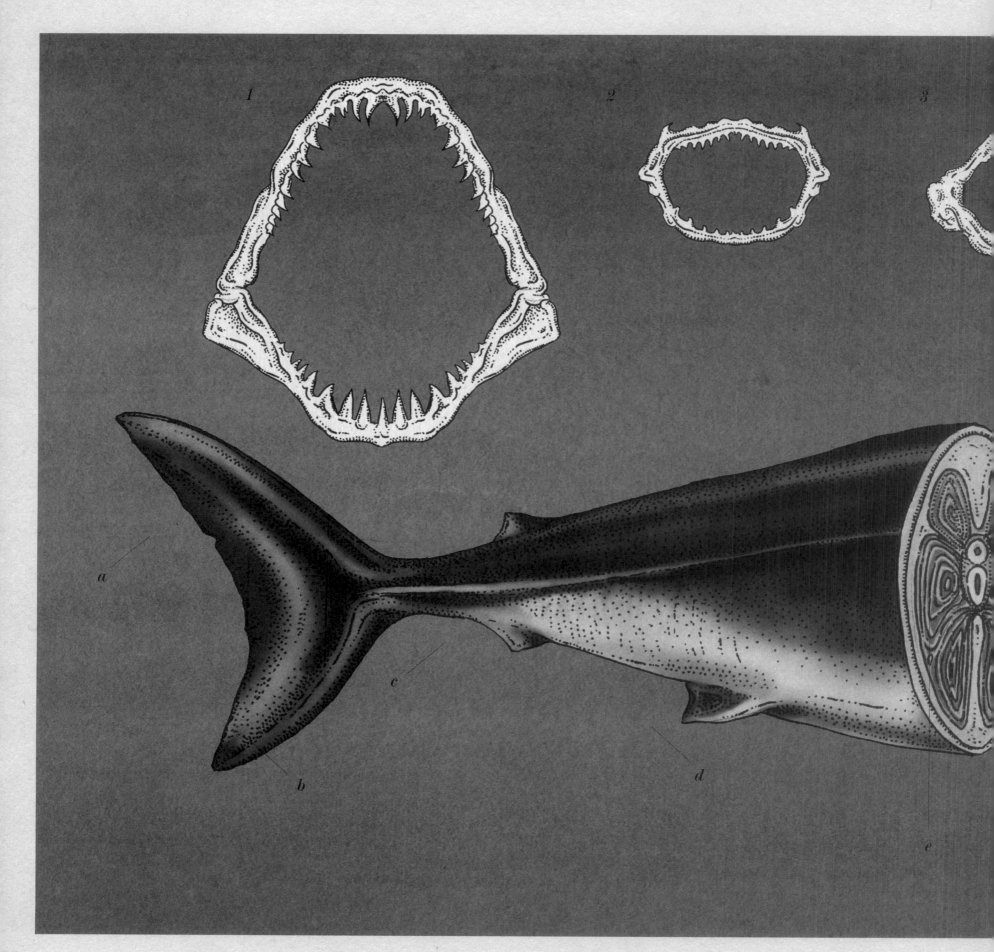

sharks cannot move backward and that if they stop moving, they begin to sink.

Sharks have very acute senses and can even detect the weak electrical signals emitted by their prey. This is called electroreception. Special blood cells keep their brains and eyes warm, giving them quick reactions. Their several sets of teeth grow constantly.

_____ *Key to plate* _____

a: Upper caudal fin

b: Lower caudal fin

c: Anal fin

d: Pelvic fin

e: Spine

f: Pectoral fin

g: Gills

h: Jaw

1: **Shortfin mako shark's jaw**
Isurus oxyrinchus
Dagger-like teeth grip fast-moving prey.

2: **Sharpnose sevengill shark's jaw**
Heptranchias perlo
Jagged upper teeth grip thrashing prey.

3: **Zebra bullhead shark's jaw**
Heterodontus zebra

Adapted to feed from the seabed.

4: **Kitefin shark's jaw**
Dalatias licha
Lower teeth form a continuous cutting edge to bite chunks from larger prey.

5: **Sandbar shark's jaw**
Carcharhinus plumbeus
Adapted to a fish-based diet.

Skates and Rays

Skates and rays are types of cartilaginous fish, making them relatives of sharks. They have long, thin tails that can be armed with a venomous stinger, wide disc-like bodies, and "wings" that they use to swim by beating them in a motion like that of a flying bird. Some species are commonly seen leaping out of the water.

To hunt, skates and rays hide on the seabed, waiting to ambush any small fish, mollusk, or crustacean that crosses their path. A skate or ray will settle its broad, flat body—which is often covered with a camouflaging pattern—on the ocean floor, then flap its wings to stir up the sand and conceal itself. Underneath the sand, the fish cannot use its eyes, so it uses its senses of smell and electroreception to locate prey, and it breathes through spiracles behind its eyes.

Predators that hunt using electroreception are able to sense the weak bioelectric field generated by their prey's nervous system. These electrical currents are extremely faint but are easier to detect underwater than on land because water is a much better electrical conductor than air.

Key to plate

1: Thornback ray
Raja clavata
Length: 33 inches/85 centimeters
This kite-shaped ray is one of the most commonly seen species, although it can be difficult to identify because coloration varies from fish to fish. It has between thirty-six and forty-four rows of teeth in its upper jaw, and its long, solid tail has thorns running down its length. Its eggs are encased in black leathery sacs, commonly known as mermaid's—or devil's—purses. It can live for up to twelve years.

2: Spotted eagle ray
Aetobatus narinari
Length: 70 inches/180 centimeters
The spotted eagle ray is typically found in shallow tropical waters. It is also known to jump out of the water,

sometimes inadvertently landing in boats. Its tail can grow more than three times its body width if left unharmed but can easily get caught and damaged in fishing nets. This ray is ovoviviparous, which means that it gives birth to live young.

3: Blonde ray
Raja brachyura
Length: 39 inches/100 centimeters
The blonde ray, named for its sandy color, can be found throughout the waters of Europe and the Mediterranean, where it is most commonly found at depths of 1,148 feet/350 meters. It has 60–90 rows of teeth and lives on a diet of small, bony fish and shrimp. It reproduces by laying horned black eggs, similar to those of the thornback ray.

4: Smooth skate
Malacoraja senta
Length: 23 inches/60 centimeters
The heart-shaped smooth skate is a relatively small species, so named because, unlike other skates, its shoulders and upper pelvic fins are not covered with rough denticles. It can be found in the waters of the northwest Atlantic.

5: Shovelnose guitarfish
Rhinobatos productus
Length: 45 inches/114 centimeters
The shape of the shovelnose guitarfish's dorsal fin led people to believe it was a shark, but it is in fact a species of ray. By day it lies on the ocean bed, covered in sand, waiting to ambush a passing victim, and by night it cruises the seabed, searching for prey.

Ray-finned Fish

Ray-finned fish account for nearly 99 percent of all species of fish. All have a jointed backbone: they were the first animals to benefit from this key evolutionary development. Their rayed fins — webbed skin supported by bony spines — allow them to make quick and complex movements, such as moving backward, that cartilaginous fish cannot. They control their depth in the water with an air-filled bladder, which they use as a buoyancy aid. By adjusting the pressure of the gas, they can rise or sink.

Most of these species reproduce by laying eggs — sometimes laying millions at a time to increase the chances of some offspring surviving. For the same reason, ray-finned fish can often be found swimming together in the thousands in large shoals, which reduces an individual's risk of being eaten by a predator. Some shoals swim in a coordinated

movement known as schooling, a technique that has to be learned by young fish, who practice together in pairs. Schooling fish need to be able to see their neighbors clearly, so they dissipate into normal shoals in the dark. Many species have marks on their bodies and tails known as lateral lines, which not only make them highly visible, but also enable them to detect changes in water pressure, helping them to remain at a certain distance from their neighbors.

Key to plate

English perch
Perca fluviatilis
Length: 24 inches/
60 centimeters
a: Spiny dorsal fin
b: Kidney
c: Spinal vertebrae

d: Soft dorsal fin
e: Caudal fin
f: Gills
g: Heart
h: Liver
i: Intestine
j: Stomach

k: Air bladder
l: Gonad
m: Anal fin
Types of tail fin
1: Lunate tail fin
Enables speed over cistances.
2: **Emarginated tail fin**

Reduces drag.
3: **Forked tail fin**
Enables speed in open water.
4: **Rounded tail fin**
Enables quick bursts of speed.
5: **Truncate tail fin**
Found in fish that stay still.

Habitat: Coral Reefs

Coral reefs can be found in warm, clear, shallow parts of the ocean floor and are colorful environments teeming with life. The reefs are hard, stony structures gradually formed over thousands—even millions—of years by tiny animals called coral polyps. Although they cover less than one percent of the world's surface, these habitats support around 25 percent of all marine species. The majority of shallow coral reefs are found in a wide band around the equator.

Coral reefs are sometimes called "the rain forests of the sea" because of the rich biodiversity that flourishes in these habitats. Over 4,000 species of fish can be found living in coral reefs, and they are among the most vibrant and varied species in the world. Their bright coloring helps the fish to camouflage themselves and confuse predators, and many keep to confined areas where they come to know every nook and cranny of the corals to hide in.

Many species of fish living in coral reefs have elongated snouts with which they probe into the coral polyps. Because they do not swim vast distances, as open-water fish do, they have not evolved to be streamlined for moving through water for long periods of time. Instead, most fish living in coral reefs have laterally flattened bodies that let them pass through confined spaces and long ray-fins that allow them to maneuver in and out of the coral.

Key to plate

1: **Banggai cardinalfish**
Pterapogon kauderni
Length: 3 inches/7.5 centimeters
This fish is most active in the morning, and feeds until sunset. Male and female cardinalfish form a pair that inhabit and defend a particular territory.

2: **Mandarinfish**
Synchiropus splendidus
Length: 2 inches/5 centimeters
This shy, slow, and passive fish hides from predators in coral. If threatened,

it can emit a bitter mucus with an unpleasant smell.

3: **French angelfish**
Pomacanthus paru
Length: 16 inches/40 centimeters
While the adult French angelfish is black and flecked with yellow, the juvenile fish has defined yellow bands, which fade as it ages.

4: **Stoplight parrotfish**
Sparisoma viride

Length: 12 inches/30 centimeters
The parrotfish feeds in coral reefs throughout the day. At night, it creates a mucous sac that acts like a sleeping bag so that predators cannot smell it.

5: **Clown anemonefish**
Amphiprion ocellaris
Length: 3 inches/7.5 centimeters
This species lives in a harem of one female and several males. If the female dies, a male clownfish can change sex to take her place.

Gallery 3

Amphibians

Amphibians
Urodela
Frogs
Habitat: Rain forests

Amphibians

Amphibians take their name from the Greek word *amphibios*, meaning "living both in water and on land." They are famed for the dramatic metamorphoses they undergo in their lifetime. The first amphibians evolved around 370 million years ago from lungfish and were the first quadrupeds, or four-footed creatures, to have jointed limbs. Approximately 10 million years later, unchallenged by predators, amphibians became the dominant animals on Earth. The climate—much warmer and swampier than today—suited them, and some amphibians grew to be bigger than modern crocodiles.

Around 250 million years ago, however, reptiles began to rise in strength and numbers. Consequently, modern-day amphibians are much smaller and fewer, falling into three major orders: urodeles, caecilians, and frogs and toads. Most species today still have four limbs, although caecilians have adapted to their burrowing lifestyle by having strong skulls and no limbs at all.

Amphibians are cold-blooded, lay jelly-like eggs, and tend to live in freshwater environments. Most have small, primitive lungs but are also able to breathe through their skin, which allows them to stay underwater without coming up for air. This allows many amphibians to go dormant in winter, slowing their bodies and passing the colder months at the bottom of a pond or other nearby water source.

Key to plate

1: Axolotl
Ambystoma mexicanum
Length: 8 inches/20 centimeters
Also known as the Mexican walking fish, this species engages in a courtship display that involves dancing a "waltz" followed by a "hula" before copulation.

2: Mandarin salamander
Tylototriton shanjing
Length: 6 inches/15 centimeters
This highly toxic amphibian is a relatively large and sturdy creature. It lightens in color with age.

3: Darwin's frog
Rhinoderma darwinii
Length: 1 inch/3 centimeters

This species was discovered by Charles Darwin in Chile. The male has an oversize vocal sac in which it rears its young.

4: Allen's worm salamander
Oedipina alleni
Length: 5 inches/13 centimeters
Native to Latin America, this species got its name because of its long, thin body. It has no lungs at all, breathing entirely through its skin.

5: Tomato frog
Dyscophus antongilii
Length: 4 inches/10 centimeters
This frog, native to Madagascar, is nocturnal, burying itself in the moist

earth during the day and emerging to hunt at night.

6: Ornate horned frog
Ceratophrys ornata
Length: 7 inches/18 centimeters
This unfriendly species has earned itself the nickname "Pac-man" as a result of its enormous size and massive mouth.

7: White's treefrog
Litoria caerulea
Length: 4 inches/10 centimeters
This adaptable species is commonly found in Australia. If threatened, it will emit a scream to scare away its potential predator.

Urodela

This family of amphibians includes salamanders and newts. Similar to other amphibians, they have smooth, moist skin, through which they absorb oxygen. (This is easier in cold water, which contains more oxygen than warm water.) This adaptation is so effective that some species do not even have lungs.

Because their skin is delicate enough to allow oxygen to pass through, it is extremely sensitive to impurities, which makes the animals vulnerable to polluted water. Scientists often count the newts in an area to determine the health of the environment.

A male salamander can undergo changes during breeding season, signaling to females that he is ready to mate. The male Alpine newt, shown here, develops a crest

that is re-absorbed into its body when it has finished mating. Also, its skin changes color, from a camouflaging brown pattern to an eye-catching blue and orange. The eggs the female lays after mating do not have a shell but instead are enclosed in a protective jelly.

Some salamanders are brightly colored year-round. This warns predators that they are toxic and dangerous to eat. Indeed, some produce a toxin so powerful that it could kill a human, though it is dangerous only if ingested.

Another notable feature of salamanders and newts is their amazing ability to regenerate (or regrow) a lost limb!

Key to plate

1: Alpine newt
Ichthyosaura alpestris
Length: 4 inches/10 centimeters
The Alpine newt lives in forested and
mountainous terrains throughout
central Europe, near freshwater
streams and ponds. It hibernates
during the cold winter months
and emerges in the spring, when it
feeds at night. The male performs
a tail-fanning dance for the female
during courtship.

Frogs

An amphibian undergoes a series of transformations—known as a metamorphosis—during its life cycle. Its physical appearance changes dramatically during this time. Most frogs hatch from large batches of eggs laid in water and spend their first days as aquatic larvae known as tadpoles. These tadpoles have tails and gills that allow them to breathe underwater, and they have a vegetarian diet.

Soon after hatching, the tadpoles start to grow lungs, four legs, and a large jaw, and their gills and tails disappear gradually in readiness for their move from water to land. Their eyes, tongues, and legs grow bigger, and—sometimes in the space of only a day—the tadpoles are transformed into insect-eating frogs.

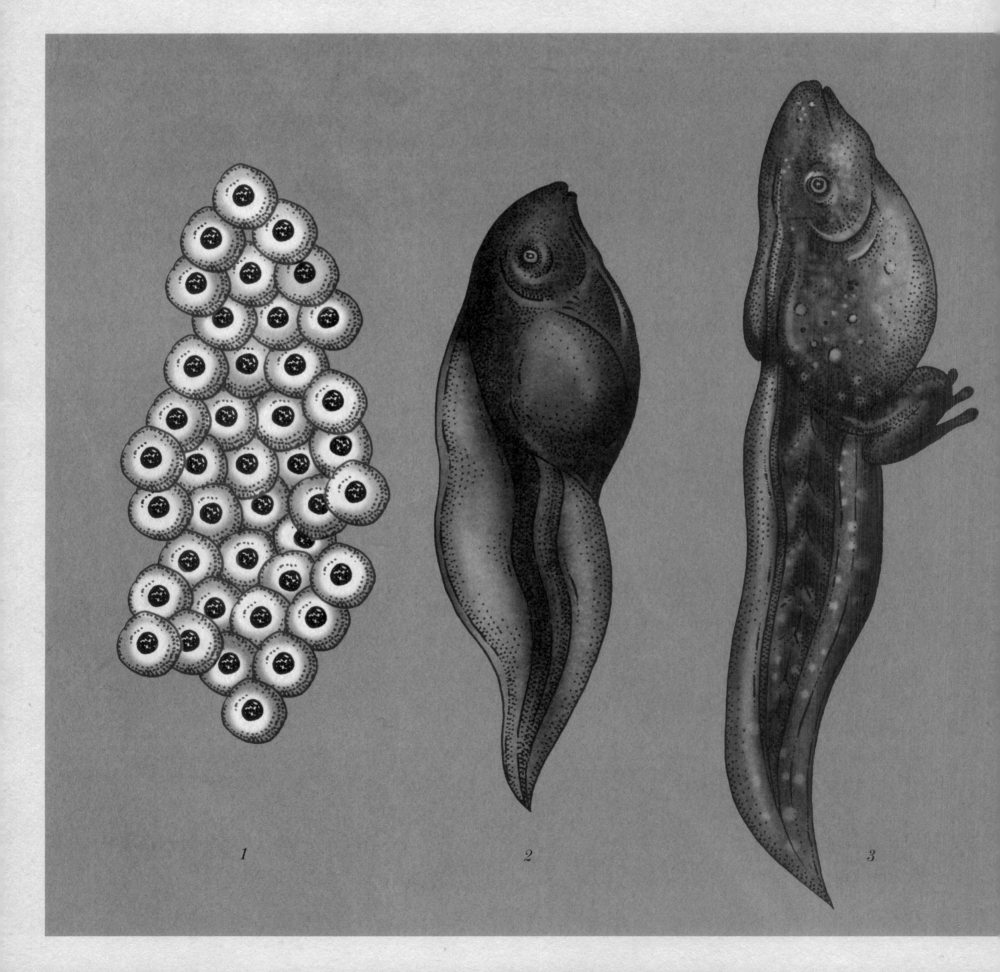

1   2   3

Many species of frogs have interesting ways of caring for their offspring. Some, such as the male Darwin's frog, nurture their young in their mouth, while others, such as the female pouched frog, allow their eggs to develop in a skin sac on their back for safety.

Most adult frogs have strong back legs that make them excellent at jumping and swimming, and some species have adapted to be able to climb and to glide through the air. They develop good hearing and loud croaks, allowing them to communicate with one another across long distances, and their skin takes on a distinctive coloring—either mottled and subdued to camouflage them or bright and colorful to ward off predators.

_____ *Key to plate* _____

European common frog
Rana temporaria
1: Frogspawn

2: Tadpole
3: Tadpole develops legs
4: Young froglet

5: Adult frog
After hatching, the development from tadpole to adult takes 12–16 weeks.

4

5

Habitat: Rain Forests

Tropical rain forests are hot, humid areas, densely populated with trees and plants due to high levels of rainfall year-round. They are located in proximity to the equator, and are thought to contain more than half of the world's plant and animal species.

Amphibians are particularly well suited to this habitat: there are more than one thousand species of frog in the Amazon basin alone. Frequent rains create a warm, swampy environment that keeps amphibians' skin moist and, therefore, breathable. As a result, many frogs are able to adopt lifestyles impossible elsewhere, living in trees and laying their eggs in leaves, safely out of reach of predators.

In order to travel from tree to tree, some frogs have developed the ability to glide. Using flaps of skin on their sides and between their toes, they stretch out as they fall through the air, allowing them to travel distances of up to 50 feet/15 meters.

Some of the best-known species of frog, such as poison-dart frogs, live in rain-forest habitats. Their brilliantly colored skin warns predators of their deadly poison, which they are able to produce by eating toxic ants.

Key to plate

1: **Blue poison-dart frog**
Dendrobates azureus
Length: 2 inches/5 centimeters
This species secretes poisons from glands all over its body. It is aggressive and will fight off those that invade its territory. The male sings to attract a female to mate with.

2: **Red-eyed treefrog**
Agalychnis cailidryas
Length: 2¹/₂ inches/6.4 centimeters
This creature's namesake red eyes are thought to have adapted because of its nocturnal lifestyle. It is an excellent climber thanks to suction cups on the underside of its feet.

3: **Waxy monkey leaf frog**
Phyllomedusa sauvagii
Length: 3 inches/7.5 centimeters
This frog lays and sandwiches its eggs in a leaf above a pond. When the tadpoles hatch, they drop into the water. It coats itself in a water-repellent secretion to reduce water loss.

4: **Granular poison-dart frog**
Oophaga granulifera
Length: 1 inch/2.5 centimeters
The male of this species is highly territorial and establishes its breeding ground by calling incessantly. The calls attract potential mates while warning other males to keep away.

5: **Cerro Pando salamander**
Bolitoglossa compacta
Length: 2¹/₂ inches/6.4 centimeters
This rarely seen salamander is moderately sized, with somewhat webbed fingers and toes. It looks after its young for an unusually long period of time — up to eight months.

6: **Thompson's caecilian**
Caecilia thompsoni
Length: 3 feet/1 meter
This limbless species is native to Colombia and is the largest of the worm-like caecilians. It burrows with its hard skull and pointed snout. It is endangered due to deforestation.

Gallery 4

Reptiles

Gila Monster

Turtles, Tortoises, and Terrapins

Snakes

Crocodiles and Alligators

Habitat: Deserts

REPTILES

Gila Monster

Reptiles evolved from amphibians nearly 320 million years ago. They were the first animals to live on land, which was possible because of scales that kept in their body moisture. Most adapted to lay shelled eggs, which sealed in water and allowed them to reproduce on land. Reptilian anatomy evolved to allow its species to walk more easily on land than amphibians, and, in fact, their name stems from the Latin word *reptilis* for "creeping."

Because of these adaptations, early reptiles had few predators and became a very successful class of animal. They grew huge in both size and number up to their apex of power as dinosaurs. For around 135 million years, dinosaurs reigned over the animal kingdom, until a mass extinction around 65 million years ago. After that, reptiles became smaller and fewer in number.

Modern reptiles share many characteristics with their dinosaur predecessors. They are cold-blooded and regulate their body temperature by moving between sun and shade. Many can shed and regenerate a limb, and some, like chameleons, can even change color. In the tree of life, reptiles form an important evolutionary link. Both birds and, later, mammals evolved from this class of animal. They are so closely linked, in fact, that modern reptiles, such as crocodiles, share more DNA with early kinds of birds than they do with lizards!

Key to plate

1: **Gila monster**
Heloderma suspectum
Length: 22 inches/56 centimeters
The Gila monster is a species of venomous lizard that lives in North America and spends most of its time

underground. It feeds mostly on eggs and small creatures often found newly born in nests, and eats only between five and ten times a year in the wild—but when it does, it devours up to one third of its body mass.

a: **Gila monster's skull and teeth**
Unlike venomous snakes, which have hollow fangs, Gila monsters have very large, grooved teeth in their lower jaw. As they bite into their prey, poison travels down the grooves.

Turtles, Tortoises, and Terrapins

Turtles are members of an order of reptiles called Testudines, which also includes tortoises and aquatic terrapins. This name refers to the hard shell that all its species possess, as a *testudo* in ancient Rome was a hard screen or shield that soldiers used to protect themselves. Little of the modern turtle's anatomy has changed from its prehistoric ancestors', who date back more than 220 million years, making turtles and tortoises more ancient than all snakes, lizards, and crocodiles.

Turtles' shells are attached to their bodies, and so their protective armor can never be taken off or left behind. Land-dwelling tortoises have higher, domed shells, while aquatic species have flatter shells. To hide inside their shells, some species fold their head alongside their shoulder, while others retract their neck and head backward. Box turtles have a hinged plate that allows their shells to close completely.

Males will often perform elaborate courtship rituals to impress females, who lay shelled eggs after mating. The temperature that the eggs are kept at affects the sex of the hatchlings (a trait shared with crocodiles and some lizards).

Key to plate

1: **Green sea turtle**
Chelonia mydas
Length: 59 inches/150 centimeters
This large sea turtle is a herbivore, feeding mostly on seagrasses. Populations of green sea turtles can be found in tropical waters of the Atlantic and Pacific Oceans.

2: **Painted turtle**
Chrysemys picta bellii
Length: 10 inches/25 centimeters
Also known as the firebelly turtle, this species spends long hours basking in the sun, particularly early in the day. It is common sight to find several painted turtles piled on top of one another, basking on a log.

3: **Blanding's turtle**
Emydoidea blandingii
Length: 8 inches/20 centimeters
This turtle has a hinge that forms a protective hatch at the front of its shell. It is omnivorous, feeding on a range of foods, including berries, fish, and frogs.

4: **Diamondback terrapin**
Malaclemys terrapin
Length: 6 inches/15 centimeters
The mild-mannered diamondback terrapin lives in brackish lagoons, tidal marshlands, and sandy beaches in east-coast America. The species nearly became extinct due to over-hunting and destruction of its habitat.

5: **Leopard tortoise**
Geochelone pardalis
Length: 19 inches/50 centimeters
The leopard tortoise is a large tortoise found in savannah habitats in Africa, where it can live for up to 100 years. Its grasping toenails make it an agile walker, strong swimmer, and surprisingly good climber.

6: **Indian star tortoise**
Geochelone elegans
Length: 11 inches/28 centimeters
The Indian star tortoise has a high tolerance to water and so can be found in places that experience a monsoon season. Its dome shape allows it to easily self-right.

Snakes

Snakes are characterized by their lack of limbs and their long, tube-like bodies. They are believed to have descended from lizards, losing their limbs in the process of evolution. Because of their narrow body shape, their paired organs, such as kidneys, are stacked one in front of the other rather than side by side, and most have just one lung. Their long and flexible backbone allows snakes an exceptional dexterity of movement.

There are around 3,400 species of snake, and they can be found on every continent except for Antarctica. All are carnivorous and possess large, flexible jaws, which allow them to eat prey much larger than their own heads. Because their teeth are designed for killing, but not chewing, they swallow their victims whole. Sometimes a snake's meal can be seen to travel down its body as it digests.

Snakes track their prey using their strong—and directional—sense of smell, which they detect with their forked tongues. Different species have their own methods of attack; around one in ten species has a venomous bite, delivered with poisonous fangs, while others use constriction, crushing prey to death by coiling their body around their victim.

―――――――――――――――― *Key to plate* ――――――――――――――――

1: Arizona coral snake
Micruroides euryxanthus
Length: 20 inches/0.5 meters
This snake can be found in scrubby, arid regions of North America. Its colorful bands warn others that it is a venomous species. In fact, its venom is similar to a cobra's, though less toxic due to its comparatively small size.

2: Paradise treesnake
Chrysopelea paradisi
Length: 4 feet/1.2 meters
Living in the forests of Southeast Asia, the paradise treesnake is an adept climber. This snake has the ability to glide from tree to tree by flattering its body and launching itself into the air from a high branch.

3: Blood python
Python curtus brongersmai
Length: 5 feet/1.5 meters
Found in tropical swamps around Indonesia, the nonvenomous blood python gets its name from its deep red coloration. When incubating her eggs, the female coils around them and shivers to keep them warm.

Crocodiles and Alligators

Crocodiles and alligators are called crocodilians as a group, and are related, having emerged around 140 million years ago from common ancestors who managed to survive extinctions that other reptiles, like dinosaurs, did not. These ancient forebears were fearsome predators, growing up to twice the length of today's crocodiles and alligators.

The modern species share their ancestors' body shape and large, fearsome jaws, containing numerous teeth. They are good swimmers, reaching speeds of more than twenty miles per hour in the water. Crocodilians are carnivorous animals and will hunt any kind of animal on land or in water. Because their jaws are designed to tear meat apart (rather than chew it), they will clamp large prey, such as a wildebeest, in their jaws and perform the "death roll," spinning prey underwater until a piece of meat comes off.

The name *crocodile* comes from the ancient Greek word *krokodilos*, meaning "worm of the stones," while the word *alligator* derives from the Spanish term *el lagarto*, meaning "lizard." Both species are sociable and vocal and can often be found grouped together and communicating with one another on riverbanks or in freshwater lakes. Female crocodilians make fierce mothers and will guard their young for up to two years.

Crocodilians have superior senses, including night vision, and receptors along their jaws that allow them to sense prey moving in water. A flap of tissue in their throat acts as a valve, allowing the animal to breathe while partly underwater by closing off its respiratory system. Because their eyes, ears, and nostrils are situated on the top of their head, they can submerge themselves in water in order to ambush prey. Their ears are so sensitive that they can hear calls from their unborn young still inside their eggs.

Key to plate

1: **Nile crocodile**
Crocodylus niloticus
Length: 16 feet/5 meters
The Nile crocodile is the second largest reptile on Earth and has a reputation as a fearsome man-eater. It is thought that up to 200 people are killed by Nile crocodiles each year.

The Nile crocodile is predominantly nocturnal, and it can sometimes be found escaping the extreme heat of the midday sun in underground burrows. It and other crocodilians have evolved to have advanced flexibility in its hip and ankle joints, giving it good mobility on land.

a: Skull
b: Shoulder bone
c: Humerus
d: Carpus and ulna
e: Ribs
f: Fibula and tibia
g: Femur
h: Caudal vertebra

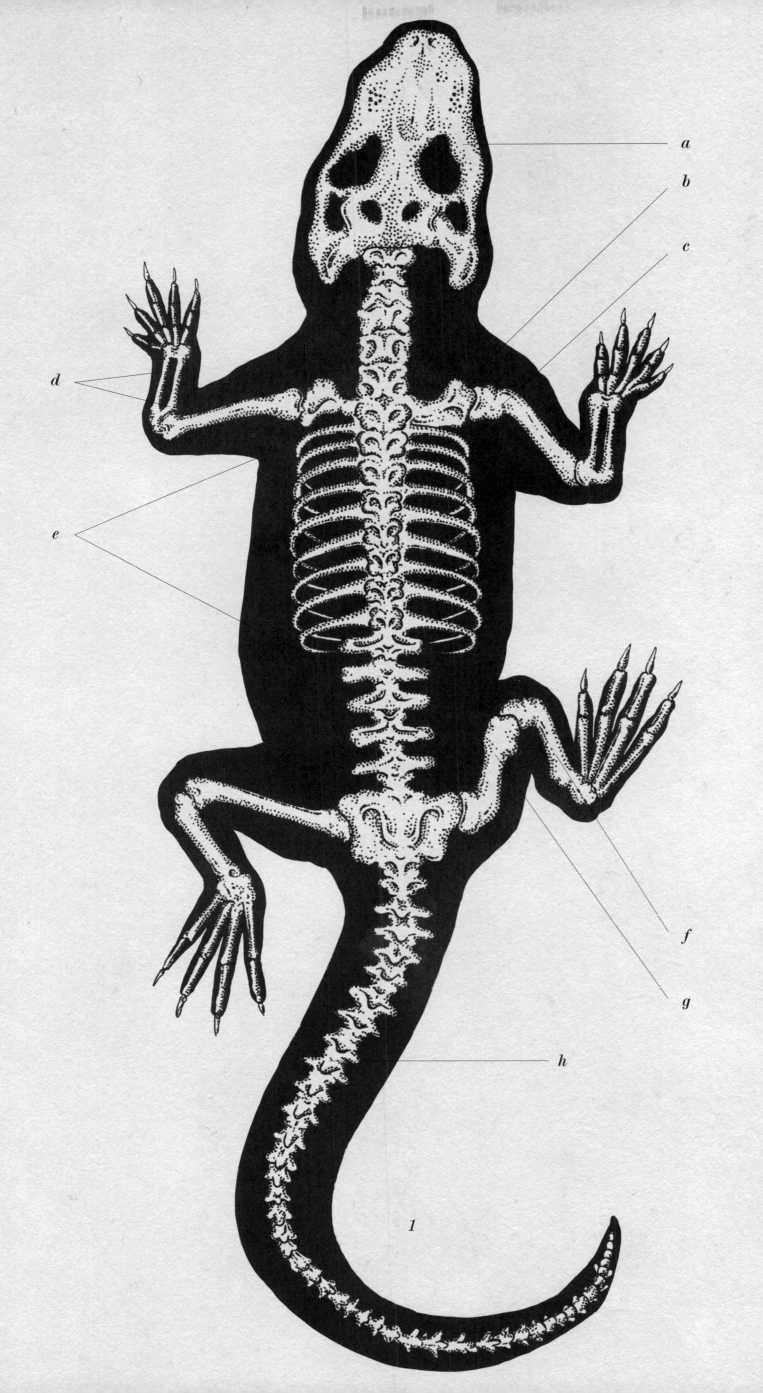

Habitat: Deserts

Deserts are areas defined by an extremely dry climate, where very little rain falls and very few plants are able to grow. Some deserts are cold, mountainous, and barren, but the largest deserts in the world are in areas where the sun is extremely hot, such as the Sahara Desert in Africa. Even in deserts that experience scorching heat by day, the temperatures can plummet at night, meaning that any species living in these habitats must cope with extreme changes in temperature.

The great highs and lows in temperature cause rocks and stones weather and break down rapidly, creating a sandy topsoil. Because of these arid conditions, few plants are able to survive and take root, which means there is little vegetation to hold the ground together. Therefore, the sands are easily blown around and sometimes form sand dunes that are sculpted by winds, creating a constantly changing landscape.

Reptiles are especially suited to living in these environments because they are able to survive with little water. One adaptation is the way a reptile might bask open-mouthed in the hot sun in order to release heat. Because reptiles cannot sweat to cool themselves, they take shelter beneath a rock during the hottest parts of the day and emerge to hunt in the evening when the sun begins to set but the sands retain enough heat to keep the animal warm.

Key to plate

1: Desert kingsnake
Lampropeltis getula splendida
Length: 4 feet/1.2 meters
This is a nonvenomous species of snake, but it is able to consume toxic creatures such as rattlesnakes due to its resistance to their venom. When threatened, it will flip onto its back and lie motionless, playing dead.

2: Baja California collared lizard
Crotaphytus vestigium
Body length: 3¹/₂ inches/9 centimeters

This creature hibernates under a rock in the cold winter months and becomes active in the warmer seasons. When running, it can become bipedal, standing up on its two hind legs.

3: Black-tailed rattlesnake
Crotalus molossus
Length: 38 inches/97 centimeters
The rattler is named for the warning sound it makes by shaking its tail when it is threatened. The venom it injects with hollow fangs stops its victim's

blood from clotting, causing the prey to bleed to death.

4: Western banded gecko
Coleonyx variegatus
Body length: 4 inches/10 centimeters
This creature is nocturnal and hunts insects, arachnids, and baby scorpions. If threatened, it curls its tail over its head to mimic a scorpion. If necessary, it can detach its tail, though because the tail stores energy resources, this strategy can be risky.

Gallery 5

Birds

Flightless Birds

Early birds evolved from tree-dwelling dinosaurs around 150 million years ago. Along with their sister group, the order Crocodilia, they were the only members from this branch of the tree of life to survive the mass extinction that killed the dinosaurs around 65 million years ago. Like ancient reptiles, early birds were carnivorous. They have since diversified and can now be found on every continent and habitat on Earth.

All birds are warm-blooded, with two legs, two wings that evolved from the reptile's forelimbs, feathers, beaks, and a lightweight skeleton. Birds reproduce sexually, like reptiles, and lay hard-shelled eggs, from which a chick hatches.

Linking reptiles to modern birds on the tree of life are a group of primitive

species called the Palaeognath, which are land-dwelling, predominantly flightless, birds. Their name comes from the Greek term meaning "old jaws," which refers to their reptile-like mouths. Their bare, scaly legs also betray their reptilian ancestry.

─────────────────── *Key to plate* ───────────────────

1: **Common ostrich**
Struthio camelus
Height: 8 feet/2.4 meters
This is the largest and fastest-running bird, reaching speeds of up to 43 miles/ 70 kilometers per hour. Its powerful legs can stride up to 16 feet/ 5 meters. Ostriches have been known to kill lions with their kick!

2: **Southern cassowary**
Casuarius casuarius
Height: 6 feet/1 8 meters
The cassowary is recognizable by its horn-like casque and two red wattles that hang from its throat. It has a dagger-like claw on its inner toe, which it uses to charge down and spear its target.

3: **Cassowary eggs**
Length: 5 inches/13 centimeters
The male cassowary incubates the egg and raises its young alone.

4: **Ostrich egg**
Length: 6 inches/15 centimeters
The largest of all bird eggs. Hens lay their eggs in the dominant hen's nest.

Penguins

Penguins can be found in coastal areas in the Southern Hemisphere and are instantly recognizable thanks to their upright stance and distinctive black and white plumage. While their coloring makes them easy to spot on land, it acts to camouflage them in water: their black backs match the ocean's darkness from above, and their white bellies blend in with the brightness of the sun and ice from below. This is known as countershading.

Penguins are fast and agile swimmers, despite being flightless and ungainly on land. Their wings and large, webbed feet have adapted to act like flippers in the water. It is thought, however, that their ancestors could indeed fly and that penguins are more closely related to the albatross than to other flightless birds.

Most species have evolved to survive in cold and harsh environments. Their feathers, densely packed and waterproof, offer excellent insulation, and their blood flow has adapted so that they do not freeze when standing on ice. Incubating an egg in these conditions is challenging, and to do this, they lay a single egg, warming it under their plumage and keeping it off the ice by balancing it on their feet. They are attentive parents, taking turns catching fish and feeding their young once hatched.

Key to plate

1: **Emperor penguin**
Aptenodytes forsteri
Height: 3 feet/1 meter
The emperor penguin is the largest of all the penguin species. It lives in Antarctica, which is one of the most inhospitable climates on Earth.

They live in huge colonies, which number tens of thousands of birds.

In order to stay warm, the penguins huddle in a group. Each bird takes a turn standing exposed to the cold winds on the outside of the cluster before rotating back inside the center for warmth and protection.

The penguins' diet consists primarily of fish. They have been known to swim distances of more than 600 miles/960 kilometers in a single foraging trip! Their body is streamlined for swimming and their feathers are covered in a waterproof oil, which keeps them dry and warm in the water.

The emperor penguin can stay submerged underwater for up to eighteen minutes at a time. Its skeleton has evolved to be solid, rather than air-filled like those of other birds, which allows it to dive to depths of up to 1,476 feet/450 meters without suffering from barotrauma, a lethal condition brought on when changes in pressure cause pockets of gas within a creature's body to expand, damaging the surrounding tissue.

The emperor penguin is famous for its reproductive cycle. It breeds during the Antarctic winter between May and June, when no other creature inhabits the region, which reduces the threat of predators.

The penguins walk up to 50 miles/80 kilometers inland, where the female lays her egg. She transfers it to her male partner, who incubates it in his brood pouch, balancing it on his feet. The female then departs, leaving the male to protect the egg from winds as fierce as 120 miles/190 kilometers per hour and temperatures as low as -40°F/-40°C. He must survive this time without food, living on stored body fat alone. Once the chick has hatched, the female returns with food for her young, releasing the male to return to the sea to feed. By this time, he will have fasted for more than three months.

1

Albatross

Learning to fly was a key evolutionary step for most birds, and scientists still aren't sure how or why they first took to the skies. Nevertheless, it has allowed them to inhabit every continent, habitat, and island on Earth. Flying birds' bodies have adapted to become perfectly suited to the task, with light skeletons made up of air-filled bones. Their long, hinged wings are covered in aerodynamic feathers, and their strong pectoral muscles allow them to flap their wings, pushing the air downward and generating lift.

The albatross is known for its masterful flying, and spends most of its life gliding above the seas, coming back to shore only in order to nest. The great albatross has the largest wingspan of any living bird, and it uses it to great effect, soaring through the skies and scouting for fish with its powerful sense of smell.

To help sustain their long flights, albatross are especially reliant on gliding, which allows them to conserve energy. When gliding, their long, curved wings slice through the air, making the air particles travel faster across the top of the wing than underneath it. This creates a lower air pressure above the bird than below, which keeps the bird aloft in a similar manner to airplanes.

―――――――――――――――― *Key to plate* ――――――――――――――――

1: **Wandering albatross**
Diomedea exulans
Wingspan: 10 feet/3 meters
This is the largest species of albatross and is found almost exclusively south of the equator. The chicks are born with brown plumage and turn white with age.

2: **Black-browed albatross**
Thalassarche melanophrys
Wingspan: 7 feet/2 meters
The young black-browed albatross has a blue beak that turns orange in adulthood. A salt gland in its nasal passage allows it to excrete any excess salt from seawater out of its body.

3: **Waved albatross**
Phoebastria irrorata
Wingspan: 7 feet/2 meters
This is the only albatross species found entirely in the tropics. It can spend six years at sea before returning to land to mate. It feeds at night, when squid swim close to the surface of the water.

Flamingos, Storks, Ibises, and Herons

With elongated legs and necks, these creatures tend to live in wetlands and are generally carnivorous, living on a variety of aquatic prey. They can be found inhabiting areas across the globe, and some species are partially migratory.

Flamingos are highly sociable creatures and live together in enormous flocks. They benefit from the vigilance of their neighbors, who keep a lookout for predators, and often rear their young together. They have adapted to survive in challenging environments and tend to inhabit lakes with high levels of salt or alkalis in the water. Their characteristic coloring derives from a type of bacteria they ingest when eating their diet of shrimp. Consequently, flamingos can range in color from off-white to a shocking coral pink. Usually, the healthier the animal, the more vibrantly colored it is, which makes its hue attractive to a mate.

Related to flamingos are storks, herons, and ibises. Herons in particular are excellent fishers, standing still and silent, waiting for prey. They have lightning-fast reactions and employ their S-shaped neck and sharp bill to spear fish with impressive speed.

Key to plate

1: **Grey-winged trumpeter**
Psophia crepitans
Height: 20 inches/52 centimeters
Named for its loud honking call, this easily tamed bird makes a good guard.

2: **American flamingo**
Phoenicopterus ruber
Height: 43 inches/109 centimeters
The flamingo buries its head to feed, sucking and filtering mud with its beak.

3: **Northern gannet**
Morus bassanus
Height: 35 inches/89 centimeters
This bird dives into water from heights of up to 131 feet/40 meters to catch fish.

4: **Brown booby**
Sula leucogaster
Height: 29 inches/74 centimeters
This seabird tracks tuna from the sky to catch small fish that flee to the surface.

5: **Western reef heron**
Egretta gularis
Height: 26 inches/65 centimeters
During courtship, this heron's dark legs take on a pinkish-red color.

6: **Black-crowned night heron**
Nycticorax nycticorax
Height: 24 inches/60 centimeters
This nocturnal hunter is the most widely distributed heron in the world.

7: **Grey-crowned crane**
Balearica regulorum
Height: 41 inches/105 centimeters
This species is known for its elaborate courtship ritual, in which it dances to impress a mate. It lives in the dry African savannahs but returns to water during the breeding season.

8: **Goliath heron**
Ardea goliath
Height: 5 feet/1.5 meters
This largest, tallest species of heron on Earth is able to walk in deeper waters than its competition, spearing prey with its sharp bill. It is commonly found in sub-Saharan Africa.

Birds of Prey

Birds of prey are also known as raptors, which comes from the Latin word *rapere*, meaning "to seize." They are carnivorous, and most have evolved into formidable hunters. Many are apex predators, meaning that they are at the top of the food chain, with no predators of their own. Some, such as the bald eagle, are so fearsome that they will hunt mammals larger than themselves, like small deer. Others, such as vultures, are scavengers and eat the flesh of animals that are already dead, called carrion, rather than hunting live prey.

Birds of prey have acute senses, sharp beaks for tearing apart flesh, and strong feet that usually feature long talons with an opposable hind claw for snatching their target from the air. They can live for an exceptionally long time, some reaching fifty years of age.

Birds of prey are typically fast and agile flyers: the peregrine falcon reaches the fastest speed of any living creature on Earth by diving toward its prey at speeds of up to 200 miles/389 kilometers per hour from high in the air. The highest flying species of bird is also believed to be a bird of prey: the Rüppel's vulture has been known to reach altitudes of up to 36,100 feet/11,000 meters.

Key to plate

1: **Secretary bird**
Sagittarius serpentarius
Wingspan: 7 feet/2 meters
The secretary bird, native to Africa, is one of the only birds of prey known to chase its prey down on foot. It has also been observed flushing out its victim by stomping on clumps of vegetation, then going in for the kill, with repeated strikes from its hard beak or blows from its strong feet. When attacking snakes, the bird uses its wings to protect itself from a venomous bite.

2: **African harrier-hawk**
Polyboroides typus
Wingspan: 5 feet/1.5 meters
The African harrier-hawk is omnivorous, eating a diet of fruits and berries as well as small vertebrates. It hunts mostly in trees and bushes, and seldom in flight. It is good at climbing and uses its wings and double-jointed legs to scramble up trees to raid other birds' nests.

3: **Ornate hawk eagle**
Spizaetus ornatus
Wingspan: 4 feet/1.2 meters
The ornate hawk eagle lives in the tropical forests of Central and South America. It can often be seen perched high at the top of a tree, scanning the ground below for prey. It hunts other birds, reptiles, and mammals, and has even been known to attack primates.

4: **Crested caracara**
Caracara plancus
Wingspan: 4 feet/1.2 meters
The crested caracara is found in open land in the southern parts of North America through Peru and Amazonian Brazil, and is a common sight on cattle ranches. It is not an agile flyer and seldom hunts for prey, opting instead to scavenge for food and feed on carrion.

5: **Bateleur**
Terathopius ecaudatus
Wingspan: 6 feet/1.8 meters
The bateleur is native to Africa. It has a unique style of flying: it rocks its wings from side to side as it glides, as though it were trying to balance. The skin on the bateleur's face and legs will flush bright red when it gets agitated. It can also puff out its crest and chest feathers and emit a barking noise uncommon among other raptors.

Exotic Birds

Tropical birds and other exotic species such as hummingbirds often display bright and colorful plumage, making them some of the most vibrantly colored creatures on Earth. During the breeding season, male birds-of-paradise perform elaborate courting rituals, displaying their decorative feathers and dancing to impress a female.

Birds are warm-blooded creatures with a fast metabolism. Their brains, therefore, have evolved to be more advanced than those of their reptilian forebears. Some species, such as macaws, are considered particularly intelligent and have been known to employ logical thought and use tools to access food that is out of reach. Their intelligence makes them social creatures, and many parrots form pairs that share a strong bond.

Hummingbirds are among the smallest birds in the animal kingdom, measuring less than 5 inches/13 centimeters long. However, they display a formidable dexterity and precision when flying. They are the only birds able to fly backward and are also able to hover in one spot in order to extract nectar from flowers. They accomplish this by flapping their wings up to eighty times a second, which creates their namesake "hum."

Toucans are known for their large and colorful bill. This bill is far from solely decorative, however. They use it to reach many fruits in a tree without needing to fly to a different branch. Their bill also helps to regulate their body temperature.

Key to plate

1: Ruby-throated hummingbird
Archilochus colubris
Length: 3¹/₂ inches/9 centimeters
Although the hummingbird is specially adapted to feed on nectar, it raises its young on insects, which are a better source of protein.

2: Greater bird-of-paradise
Paradisaea apoda
Length: 17 inches/43 centimeters
This is the largest species of bird-of-paradise, famous for its elaborate ritual mating dance, in which it displays its colorful plumes.

3: Ruby-topaz hummingbird
Chrysolampis mosquitus
Length: 3 inches/8 centimeters

This species can be found in tropical South America. Its bill is shorter than that of other hummingbirds.

4: Rose-ringed parakeet
Psittacula krameri
Length: 16 inches/40 centimeters
The rose-ringed parakeet has the widest distribution of any parrot species: it is found from West Africa to Southeast Asia to areas in Europe.

5: Rosy-faced lovebird
Agapornis roseicollis
Length: 7 inches/18 centimeters
Native to southwest Africa, this sociable bird can often be spotted sleeping with its face turned toward its neighbor.

6: Mallee ringneck parrot
Barnardius barnardi macgillivrayi
Length: 13 inches/33 centimeters
The smallest and least aggressive of the Australian ringneck parrots, the mallee can live for fifteen years.

7: Red-breasted toucan
Ramphastos dicolorus
Length: 17 inches/43 centimeters
This is the smallest member of the toucan family. Its impressively large bill is relatively light.

8: Galah
Eolophus roseicapilla
Length: 14 inches/35 centimeters
This species is one of the most common cockatoos in Australia.

Owls

All owls are carnivorous and have evolved to hunt in the dark. They have distinctive round, flat faces with small beaks and large eyes that allow them to see well in poorly lit conditions. Owls are masters of the surprise attack. The patterns on their feathers allow them perfect camouflage to blend in with their surroundings in dim conditions, and their feathers have also adapted to muffle the sound of their wings, making them near-silent flyers.

Owls' eyes are located at the front of their head, giving them two overlapping fields of vision. This means that they can accurately determine their exact distance from their prey. The unusual size and shape of their eyes means that owls cannot move them in their sockets, as humans do. As a result, owls have developed flexible necks in order to turn their heads and change their view. Some can rotate their head up to 270 degrees!

Owls also have an extremely acute sense of hearing thanks to a pair of ears that are located at slightly uneven heights on either side of their head. This uneven placement allows the owl to discover the exact direction a sound is coming from. This directional hearing is the most accurate of any animal species.

Key to plate

1: Barn owl
Tyto alba
Wingspan: 43 inches/109 centimeters
The barn owl is the most common of all species of owl and can be found on every continent except for Antarctica. Its name comes from its tendency to nest in buildings. It can be found living in both urban and rural environments.

Barn owls have excellent night vision and directional hearing, which allows them to detect creatures hidden from sight underground or beneath snow—a useful ability that allows them to hunt in deepest winter.

When breeding, the female takes sole responsibility for incubating the eggs, during which time the male hunts and delivers meat and grubs to her.

2: Spectacled owl
Pulsatrix perspicillata
Wingspan: 33 inches/85 centimeters
Found primarily in the rain forests of Central and South America, the spectacled owl is named for its dramatic white eyebrows that frame its eyes, giving the impression that it is wearing glasses.

It is a solitary creature, roosting alone in a tree by day and hunting by night. It is most vocal under the cover of darkness and makes a distinctive knocking or tapping sound.

The female spectacled owl emits a high-pitched scream, which has been likened to a steam engine.

It feeds on insects, birds, and amphibians and will occasionally hunt larger creatures such as skunks.

3: Southern white-faced owl
Ptilopsis granti
Wingspan: 27 inches/70 centimeters
This small—and rarely seen—species of owl is found in a variety of habitats in sub-Saharan Africa, from woodland to open savannah.

It has been nicknamed the "transformer owl" thanks to the unique displays it puts on when threatened. If approached by an opponent slightly bigger than itself, it puffs up its feathers, attempting to seem larger. When faced with a much bigger predator, it flattens and sucks its feathers into its body, hides behind its wing, and squints to camouflage itself against a tree.

It occupies other birds' nests and will even evict the current occupants!

1

2

3

Habitat: Woodlands

Woodland habitats are made up of trees, shrubs, and grasses; the greater the variety of plants growing, the more animals it can support as a habitat. Some woodlands are deciduous, meaning that the trees change with the seasons, shedding their leaves in the winter and growing new foliage in the spring. Others are evergreen, keeping their leaves year-round.

Many species of bird live in woodlands for at least some of the year. Some of the world's best-known songbirds can be found in this habitat; you can tell them apart by their complex and unique songs. Birds sing for lots of reasons: to assert their territory, attract a mate, or alert others to danger.

In areas where the woodland is deciduous, many species take part in an annual migration. They live and breed among green trees during the summer, then fly thousands of miles south when the weather turns colder and the leaves begin to fall to find food and warmer weather. This is a dangerous and exhausting journey, and most birds travel in large flocks, seeking safety in numbers.

Key to plate

1: Stock dove
Columba oenas
Length: 12¹/₂ inches/33 centimeters
Doves and pigeons belong to the same family. The stock dove is the largest and rarest of all doves, and the most geographically dispersed.

2: Eurasian blackbird
Turdus merula
Length: 10 inches/25 centimeters
This is a species of true thrush. It is able to send one half of its brain to sleep at one time, which allows it to remain alert during migration.

3: Eurasian nuthatch
Sitta europaea
Length: 6 inches/15 centimeters
This species' name derives from its habit of wedging nuts into gaps in trees, then hacking them open.

4: House sparrow
Passer domesticus
Length: 6¹/₂ inches/16 centimeters
The house sparrow is a very social bird known to share dust baths and indulge in social singing. It coexists happily alongside humans.

5: European starling
Sturnus vulgaris
Length: 8¹/₂ inches/22 centimeters
The starling is a gregarious bird that lives in huge, noisy flocks. It is known for its beautiful flocking displays at sunset.

6: Blue tit
Cyanistes caeruleus
Length: 5 inches/13 centimeters
The small blue tit lives on an insect-based diet. The yellowness of its belly indicates the number of yellow and green caterpillars it has eaten.

7: Song thrush
Turdus philomelos
Length: 9 inches/23 centimeters
The song thrush, named for its melodious voice, eats snails by smashing their shells with a stone. It migrates by cover of darkness at night.

Gallery 6

Mammals

Marsupials

Mammals are the most recent animals to appear on the tree of life. They evolved from reptiles, and egg-laying monotremes, like the duck-billed platypus, demonstrate the evolutionary link between mammals and reptiles. Today, mammals dominate life on Earth.

Mammals have hair or fur and are warm-blooded, which allows them to maintain a constant body temperature in any climate. Mammals give birth to live young, which they feed with their own milk. Most mammals have four limbs, a tail, and a relatively large brain, which allows some species the benefit of unprecedented mental capacity and complexity of thought. Developing high levels of intelligence takes time and experience, and so mammals rely on their nurturing parents for a comparatively long time as they grow.

Marsupials are pouched mammals and can be found in Australia, New Zealand, New Guinea, nearby islands, and in the Americas. Their young are born earlier than other mammals and are carried in the mother's pouch, where they are nourished by her milk. As mammals were evolving, Earth's landmasses were gradually moving into the positions where our continents are located today. Marsupials were originally found in South America around 50 million years ago, but they traveled to Antarctica by land, from where, at that time, Australia was only a short stretch of water away. Australia has been geographically isolated since then, which explains why the mammals found there today are so unique.

Key to plate

1: Red kangaroo
Macropus rufus
Body length: 48 inches/123 centimeters
The largest species of marsupial, this kangaroo is robustly built, with a tail strong enough to support its entire body weight. To avoid overheating in the Australian sun, it licks its wrists.

2: Striped possum
Dactylopsila trivirgata
Body length: 10 inches/25 centimeters
The possum is nocturnal and forages for grubs and probes for termites with its elongated fourth claw. It drums bark with its feet to locate hidden wood-boring insects. Like a skunk, it can emit a foul stench.

3: Common spotted cuscus
Spilocuscus maculatus
Body length: 16 inches/40 centimeters
The male is rust-colored and spotted, while the female has creamy tan fur. This shy nocturnal creature lives in the tropical rain forests and dense mangroves of Australasia and lives almost entirely in trees. It is equipped with strong grasping fingers and toes for its arboreal life.

4: Sugar glider
Petaurus breviceps
Body length: 7 inches/18 centimeters
This small, soft-furred possum has a thin membrane that stretches from its wrists and its ankles and acts as a parachute, allowing it to glide from tree to tree. Its long bushy tail helps it to balance and direct itself in midair, and its large claws give it excellent grip.

5: Koala
Phascolarctos cinereus
Body length: 29 inches/74 centimeters
This creature spends most of its life in trees, out of danger from predators. Its diet of eucalyptus leaves is so nutritionally incomplete that a koala spends much of its day sleeping to conserve energy. Eucalyptus leaves are hard to digest and toxic. Mother koalas feed their young their own feces, because the mother's digestive process filters out the toxins.

MAMMALS

Elephants

Elephants were once part of a much larger family that also included mammoths, but currently all but two kinds are extinct. Even these surviving species of elephant are threatened by humankind's poaching of their ivory and destruction of their habitats.

On the tree of life, elephants are most closely related to manatees, and it is thought that millions of years ago they lived predominantly in water, using their trunk as a snorkel. Even today, they remain strong swimmers.

Overheating is a problem for elephants, as they have not evolved to sweat like some other mammals. To counter this, if an elephant begins to overheat, blood travels to its large, flat ears. Its ears flap in the breeze, cooling the blood, which then circulates back through its body, cooling the entire animal.

Elephants are currently the largest animals living on land. Despite their massive size and weight, they are surprisingly quiet when walking, thanks to shock-absorbing tissues in their feet, which also help them remain sure of foot.

―――――――――――――――― *Key to plate* ――――――――――――――――

1: Asian elephant
Elephas maximus
Height: 8½ feet/2.6 meters
The Asian elephant has smaller ears and a more arched back than its African cousins. It also has smaller tusks, if it has any at all.

A female Asian elephant is able to breed at around age fourteen, and she may be ready to mate at any time of the year. The mother carries her single unborn calf for up to twenty-two months. The newborn is dependent on its mother for up to forty-eight months, which means that the female elephant is able to reproduce only once every three or four years at most.

The Asian elephant is such a large creature that it needs to consume around 300 pounds/136 kilograms of food in a single day to sustain itself.

This species has teeth that move forward inside its mouth as it ages, which is unusual for a mammal. Their teeth wear down with use and are replaced by the set behind. However, with only limited sets available, if all its teeth are used in its lifetime, it can starve to death.

Primates

Primates are thought to have evolved between 65 and 85 million years ago. They are made up of two groups: the mostly nocturnal Strepsirrhini, which includes lemurs, lorises, and bushbabies; and the Haplorhini, which includes apes, monkeys, and *Homo sapiens* (human beings). The word *primate* derives from the Latin word *primas*, meaning "of the first rank," while *Homo sapiens* derives from the Latin for "wise man."

Primates have four limbs, each with five digits, and most have a tail, which offers extra stability in treetops. They have forward-facing eyes to help them to judge distances when swinging from branch to branch, and, unlike most other animals, primates can see a large spectrum of color. They are most notably characterized by their large brain, which makes them highly intelligent and sociable.

About 2.3 million years ago, primates began to stand and walk on two feet. They displayed a highly developed intellect through their use of tools and ability to create fire. Modern humans evolved around 200,000 years ago. This makes us one of the youngest species on Earth. The earliest modern humans were found in southwestern Africa, and people all over the world share a common ancestry with our forebears there.

Key to plate

1: De Brazza's monkey
Cercopithecus neglectus
Length: 24 inches/62 centimeters
This monkey is native to the forests of central Africa. Its large feet allow it to roam the forest floor more successfully than other primates. It is a sociable and communicative creature, imparting information visually, vocally, and via touch.

2: Golden lion tamarin
Leontopithecus rosalia
Length: 13 inches/33 centimeters
This monkey's prehensile tail means that it is suited to life in trees, eating flowers, nectar, and eggs. It forms strong bonds with members of its group—it shares food and jointly cares for another tamarin's offspring.

3: Guereza
Colobus guereza
Length: 23 inches/60 centimeters
The guereza is found in equatorial regions of Africa and lives in groups of up to fifteen individuals. It spends the majority of its time in the branches of trees, but it does come down to the forest floor to feed. At night, a sentry watches for predators.

4: Mandrill
Mandrillus sphinx
Length: 31 1/2 inches/80 centimeters
The playful mandrill is one of the largest species of monkey in the world and lives in the tropical rain forests of Africa. It spends its days foraging on the forest floor and returns to the trees to sleep.

5: Common chimpanzee
Pan troglodytes
Length: 53 inches/135 centimeters
The chimpanzee is one of humankind's closest relatives and shares 98 percent of our genes. These highly intelligent animals live in groups of up to 150 individuals in forested regions of Gabon, Cameroon, and the Democratic Republic of the Congo.

6: Black-crested mangabey
Lophocebus aterrimus
Length: 22 inches/56 centimeters
The black-crested mangabey, found in Angola and the Democratic Republic of the Congo, has a distinctive "whoop-gobble" call with which it defends its territory. Deforestation has placed this species under threat.

Rodents

Rodents are an extraordinarily successful kind of mammal; they have flourished in vastly different environments and can be found in great numbers all around the world. Counting rats, mice, squirrels, hamsters, porcupines, and beavers among their ranks, they make up around 40 percent of all mammal species.

Some rodents, such as mice, are prolific breeders, which partly explains why there are so many of them on Earth! They become sexually mature early in their lives and are able to reproduce year-round. They have short gestation periods, give birth to multiple live young, and have to wait only a short period of time for their young to become

independent before they are able to mate again. Thus, it is possible for one mouse to give birth to over 100 young in a single year!

All rodents have sharp front teeth that never stop growing, which means that they must frequently gnaw on things to stop the teeth from growing too long.

Key to plate

1: Northern Luzon giant cloud rat
Phloeomys pallidus
Body length: 16 inches/40 centimeters
This Philippine rat lives in treetops.

2: Long-eared jerboa
Euchoreutes naso

Body length: 3 inches/7.5 centimeters
Native to the Gobi Desert, this rodent performs high leaps to catch insects.

3: Lowland paca
Cuniculus paca
Body length: 28 inches/70 centimeters

Paca means "alert" in the Tupi language, spoken in Brazil, where this species lives.

4: Prevost's squirrel
Callosciurus prevostii
Body length: 9¹/₂ inches/24 centimeters
This squirrel lives in Asian rain forests.

Bats

Bats are the only mammals to have evolved to fly. Skin stretched across their forelimbs and down their extended digits forms wings that are much thinner than those of birds and allow bats to maneuver more quickly and accurately in the air.

Bats are mostly nocturnal creatures, sleeping through the day, often wrapping their wings around themselves for warmth. They come out to hunt at twilight, when there is less competition from other predators for the same food sources. They eat a variety of things, including a large quantity of insects, and sometimes—in the case of the vampire bat—they even suck blood from large mammals!

Bats can detect prey and navigate in complete darkness thanks to echolocation, an ability they share with some other mammals such as dolphins and whales. They build a detailed image of their surroundings by sending out high-pitched sound pulses and deducing from the time that noise takes to echo back what is located nearby. When it rains, however, the falling raindrops interfere with the sound pulses, meaning they cannot navigate by echolocation, so they do not come out to hunt.

Key to plate

1: Indian flying fox
Pteropus giganteus
Wingspan: 53 inches/135 centimeters
This large nocturnal bat, also known as the greater Indian fruit bat, can be found in tropical regions of south-central Asia. It rests in trees with several hundred fellow bats. The height of a male's position in a tree can indicate his hierarchical position within the group.

2: Brown long-eared bat
Plecotus auritus
Wingspan: 9 inches/23 centimeters
This species is commonly found in the U.K. and across mainland Europe. Its ears match its body in size, giving it an excellent sense of hearing that helps it to locate moths, earwigs, and other insects in the dark. It has adapted to roost in small colonies in buildings as well as trees.

3: Seba's short-tailed bat
Carollia perspicillata
Wingspan: 12 inches/30 centimeters
Found in the forests of Central and South America, this gregarious bat lives in colonies of up to one hundred individuals. It eats several varieties of fruit and is an important distributor of seeds, dispersing up to 2,500 per night in its droppings. When food is lacking, it falls into a sleep-like state of torpor.

4: Diadem roundleaf bat
Hipposideros diadema
Wingspan: 20 inches/52 centimeters
This is the most commonly found species of leaf-nosed bats, found from Australia to Southeast Asia. It roosts in caves and hollow trees and hunts by hanging from a perch and snatching passing insects such as large moths.

5: Yellow-winged bat
Lavia frons
Wingspan: 14 inches/35 centimeters
This species of bat lives throughout the savannahs and woodlands of central Africa. It is a monogamous species and can be seen engaging in courtship rituals in which the male and female circle each other. Once paired, each takes turns throughout the day to protect the roost and keep a lookout for any potential dangers.

Cats

Cats originated around 25 million years ago in Asia. While modern cats can be found in rain forests and mountainous terrains, many of the best-known big cats, such as lions and cheetahs, live in open grasslands. They are carnivores with athletic bodies and are famous for their stealth and speed: the fastest creature on land is the cheetah, which can reach speeds of up to 64 miles/104 kilometers per hour.

Cats have good eyesight, even in dim light. Their senses of hearing and smell are sensitive, and their whiskers pick up sensory information to help them hunt at dusk. In order to stay hidden, many cats have coats that are camouflaged with spots or stripes to blend into the light and shadows of their surroundings.

1

When stalking prey, cats crouch low and move forward slowly until the last moment, when, in a flash of speed, they run down their victim and snatch it with their strong claws and sharp teeth.

Domestic cats are descended from wild cats, appearing relatively recently, around 10,000 years ago. They still show their hunting abilities today, catching millions of birds and small mammals every year.

───────────────── *Key to plate* ─────────────────

1: Clouded leopard
Neofelis nebulosa
Length: 35 inches/89 centimeters
This species is excellent at climbing and is under threat due to the

deforestation (at the fastest rate on Earth) of its habitat in Southeast Asia.

2: Lion
Panthera leo

Length: 9.3 feet/2.9 meters
Second only to the tiger in size, this big cat is immediately recognizable thanks to its mane. It lives in prides where the females hunt together for food.

2

Hoofed Mammals

Hoofed mammals vary widely, from the huge and powerful rhinoceros to the elegant gazelle. Despite differences in appearance, hoofed mammals all have toes strengthened by a thick, horny covering, which never stops growing, similar to toenails. It gets worn down by constant use.

Many have horns or antlers made of bone protruding from their head, which they use to defend themselves from predators. Some species, such as deer, will demonstrate their strength and superiority by locking horns with a rival, hoping to impress a female and win the right to mate with her.

Typically, hoofed mammals are grazing herbivores, eating a diet based on shoots and leaves. They have wide, flat teeth suited to grinding down vegetation, and most have multi-chambered stomachs, which extract the maximum nutrition available from their difficult-to-digest food sources. Often, these animals regurgitate partly digested food, called cud, into their mouths, which they chew further and swallow again.

Some, such as wildebeests and bison, move in huge migratory herds, traveling thousands of miles every year to find new grazing pastures as the weather changes through the seasons and food sources become scarce.

Key to plate

1: Hippopotamus
Hippopotamus amphibius
Height: 5 feet/1.5 meters
The African hippopotamus, whose name derives from the ancient Greek for "river horse," wallows in water by day and grazes at night on grassy pastures. It lives in pods of up to thirty animals and is an aggressive creature, holding its own against crocodiles.

2: Indian rhinoceros
Rhinoceros unicornis
Height: 6 feet/1.8 meters
The Indian rhino is a smaller relative of the better-known white rhinoceros. Its single horn is smaller than that of its cousin, and it has heavy folds of thick skin with wart-like bumps on its behind. Although generally a solitary creature, it shows friendly behavior toward other rhinoceroses, bobbing its head and rubbing noses in greeting.

3: Reeves's muntjac deer
Muntiacus reevesi
Height: 17 inches/43 centimeters
This small, stocky deer originated in China but now thrives in forests around Europe since being introduced in the early twentieth century. It has short antlers, which can regrow if damaged, and prominent canine teeth.

4: Gerenuk
Litocranius walleri
Height: 36 inches/92 centimeters
The East African gerenuk has evolved to have long legs and an elongated neck, allowing it to eat leaves from the tops of shrubs and bushes that other species cannot reach. If threatened by a predator, it turns and flees, galloping away at a high speed.

5: Masai giraffe
Giraffa camelopardalis tippelskirchi
Height: 18 feet/5.5 meters
The African Masai giraffe is the tallest land mammal on Earth. Its long legs and neck have evolved to allow it to feed from the treetops, and its long and flexible tongue extends to gather twigs and leaves. When competing for a mate, males duel by battering one another with their long necks.

Sirenia, Pinnipedia, and Cetacea

Sirenia is the order to which manatees belong. They are the closest living relatives of elephants. Pinnipeds are commonly known as seals and are semi-aquatic carnivorous mammals, related to bears and wolves. Cetaceans, including whales and dolphins, are closely related to hoofed mammals, such as hippopotamuses. The largest creature ever to have existed on Earth—the blue whale—is in the order Cetacea. All have evolved to live in water, with limbs that have adapted into flippers and a tail.

Despite spending the majority of their lives underwater, these creatures have retained their mammalian need to breathe air into their lungs. As a result, they have become excellent at holding their breath—some can last for up to thirty minutes without needing to resurface. Whales and dolphins take air in and expel carbon dioxide out through a blowhole located at the top of their head.

Water-based mammals share with bats the ability to locate prey and navigate through murky water by using echolocation. Because water carries sound waves better than air, some creatures are able to communicate vocally across long distances: when humpback whales "sing" to one another, their low-frequency sounds can travel up to 10,000 miles/16,000 kilometers.

─────────────── *Key to plate* ───────────────

1: Humpback whale
Megaptera novaeangliae
Length: 46 feet/14 meters
The humpback whale is often seen breaching the water and slapping its tail. It communicates with other whales with its loud and complex song.

2: Amazonian manatee
Trichechus inunguis
Length: 8 feet/2.4 meters
Like elephants, this herbivorous creature has a constantly replenishing set of teeth. It spends much of its day asleep.

3: Narwhal
Monodon monoceros
Length: 15 feet/4.5 meters
The narwhal has a long, spiraled tusk. Its specialized diet of Arctic sealife makes it especially vulnerable to the North Pole's changing climate.

4: Short-beaked common dolphin
Delphinus delphis
Length: 6 feet/1.8 meters
This intelligent and sociable animal lives in groups of hundreds, if not thousands, of other dolphins. It is known for its aerial acrobatics.

5: Weddell seal
Leptonychotes weddellii
Length: 10 feet/3 meters
This relatively large and common species of seal is typically found around the South Pole. It can stay submerged for up to eighty minutes.

6: Walrus
Odobenus rosmarus
Length: 9$^1/_2$ feet/2.9 meters
The walrus has prominent tusks, which can grow up to 3 feet/1 meter long. It uses these tusks to compete for a mate.

Habitat: Arctic Tundra

Around the North Pole is a cold, barren area called the tundra. This habitat's freezing temperatures, high winds, lack of shelter, and scarcity of food and water make it one of the most difficult places to survive on Earth. The ground is permanently frozen (a condition known as permafrost), which makes it difficult for trees and plants to grow. This means there is little vegetation for animals to feed on.

Cold-blooded reptiles and amphibians are not at all suited to this environment, but mammals can survive because they are warm-blooded and have evolved to grow warm furry coats that keep them from freezing. The thick coat of some Arctic animals changes color through the seasons for camouflage, turning white for the snowy winter and a darker color through the summer.

Staying warm in such a cold habitat uses a lot of energy, and consequently many of these mammals, such as the Arctic wolf and polar bear, are carnivorous predators, feeding on protein-rich meat.

Polar bears are perfectly adapted to living in the icy tundra around the North Pole. They are classed as aquatic mammals and are master swimmers, able to travel up to 200 miles/322 kilometers in water. Their white coat is made up of clear, hollow hairs that keep them warm in the Arctic water and dry out quickly when they are back on land.

Key to plate

1: **Polar bear**
Ursus maritimus
Length: 7 feet/2 meters
As the Arctic ice melts in the spring and freezes in winter, the polar bear travels far and wide in search of food. It has been known to cover territories of 620 miles/1,000 kilometers from north to south. To protect its paws on the ice, the soles of its feet are furred.

2: **Muskox**
Ovibos moschatus
Length: 7 feet/2 meters

The sociable muskox lives in small groups of five or six in the summer, when food is plentiful and the weather is mild. In winter, these groups form large herds of up to sixty creatures for warmth and protection.

3: **Arctic wolf**
Canis lupus arctos
Length: 3 feet/1 meter
The Arctic wolf lives in a family pack with a defined social hierarchy; the alpha pair—who are often the parents of those lower down in the

pack's hierarchy—are at the top. The pack works together to hunt and care for any young pups.

4: **Arctic hare**
Lepus arcticus
Length: 22 inches/56 centimeters
The Arctic hare eats woody plants, buds, and grasses and uses its keen sense of smell to find food that is buried beneath the snow. It is fast and agile and can escape its predators by running at speeds of up to 40 miles/64 kilometers per hour.

Library

Index

Curators

Katie Scott studied illustration at Brighton University in England, and has since worked with the BBC, the *New York Times,* and Universal Records. She lives and works in London.

Jenny Broom studied at the Slade School of Art in London. She is an experienced editor and has written several books for children. She lives in London.

To Learn More

All About Birds
An online guide to birds and bird-watching by the Cornell Lab of Ornithology
www.allaboutbirds.org/

ARKive
A compendium of life on Earth created by Wildscreen, a conservation organization based in England
www.arkive.org/

BBC Nature: Wildlife
Includes an explorable tree of life, at www.bbc.co.uk/nature/life

Monterey Bay Aquarium
Profiles of marine creatures, from anemones to zebra sharks
www.montereybayaquarium.org/

National Geographic
Animal profiles and articles about conservation efforts
www.nationalgeographic.com/